MW01236270

SBIR Basics:
The Numbers
(Accounting, Costs, Rates, Audits, and More)

Lea A. Strickland, MBA CMA CFM CBM

Bloomington, IN  Milton Keynes, UK

authorHOUSE®

AuthorHouse™
1663 Liberty Drive, Suite 200
Bloomington, IN 47403
www.authorhouse.com
Phone: 1-800-839-8640

AuthorHouse™ UK Ltd.
500 Avebury Boulevard
Central Milton Keynes, MK9 2BE
www.authorhouse.co.uk
Phone: 08001974150

Disclaimer
This book is meant as guidance and not as a substitute for specific legal,
tax, accounting, or other business advisory services based upon the specific
operations, structures, policies, and procedures of your business.

The content of this book is based upon current information available on the SBIR program, the
agencies participating in SBIR activities and programs, and the existing legislation, regulations,
agency guidelines, and other documents available at the time of writing and publication.

First published by AuthorHouse 4/9/2007

ISBN: 978-1-4343-0768-2 (sc)

Library of Congress Control Number: 2007902570

Printed in the United States of America
Bloomington, Indiana

This book is printed on acid-free paper.

This book is dedicated to the innovators,
the entrepreneurs, and their teams.

Many thanks to my editor, Anne Harttree.

Contents

Preface

Welcome to the world of Small Business Innovation Research (SBIR), this important federal funding program is designed to provide investment in the advance of innovation in technology – biotech, infotech, defense, security, life science, learning, energy, and other existing and emerging fields of research. This is the mission of the SBIR program:

- Provide funds to small businesses for proof of concept and product development to advance innovation
- Advance technology through programs and projects to ensure that technology innovations, systems, products, and companies are available to meet the growing needs of the United States and its agencies
- Stimulate economic growth through early stage funding of "high risk" technology ideas which may lead to the expansion of jobs, tax bases, and other local, regional, and national competitive advancements.

Whether you are a first-time SBIR recipient or have been part of the SBIR process for a number of years, then this book is for you. Too often, SBIR recipients focus solely on the execution of the technical or program aspects and fail to understand and address the financial and administrative requirements – the business side – of receiving, using, managing, reporting, and complying with the requirements associated with federal funding. The consequence of this imbalance includes audit issues, lack of commercial success due to an inability to fund and produce the technology, and missed opportunities to obtain government procurement contracts.

This series will cover the "major" categories of things SBIR recipients need to understand: key terms, core policies, accounting, audit, intellectual property, and those business processes and financial controls you are expected to have in place when receiving federal funding. Doing business with government funding means more than advancing your technology, it also means advancing the business processes and management systems to ensure that the dollars you receive are expended within established program parameters. This is the world you have entered.

This book, the first in a series entitled <u>SBIR Basics – Doing Business with Government Funding</u>, is about "the numbers" – understanding accounting, costs, audits, recordkeeping, and timekeeping. It also provides a glossary of acronyms and terms. It is by no means a comprehensive look at all aspects of the requirements, but serves as an introduction, a starting point for understanding some of the administrative and financial systems requirements.

Introduction

Many years ago when I became the corporate controller and top financial person for an early-stage technology company, I "discovered" grant accounting and government funding compliance when the government auditors showed up to conduct an audit. The company was ten years old and, from its inception, had been a grant recipient for the Department of Defense, National Institutes of Health, National Science Foundation, and many other agencies. It had received millions of dollars in grants and had never been audited. The accounting system and financial controls were nowhere near the level required to satisfy governmental requirements. There were essentially no formal policies and no verifiable controls on cash management, procurement, or fixed assets. The issues extended beyond accounting into recordkeeping, timekeeping, and information systems and data security.

As with many early stage companies and start-ups, the full scope of business and accounting requirements wasn't understood and consequently wasn't addressed. The business implications and the liability to the company and its owners and officers weren't fully understood either. Fortunately, by not trying to skirt responsibility, we were able to develop a plan, implement it under the watchful eyes of the auditors, and put in place a new accounting system, develop internal controls, and satisfy the multitude of business requirements. It took time, people, and investment. It took research, analysis, and effort to find all the bits and pieces which that particular business had to meet.

No single solution or set of tools is appropriate to every company. There are a core set of principles and key concepts which, once understood, enable the recipient to create a framework for compliance. The framework and business practices which are created to deal with the requirements are the procedures, practices, and controls that successful business implement in order to focus the organization on its core activities, direct its resources, and achieve growth.

Auditors, as well as the regulations and compliance they enforce, are protection of our tax dollars. The federal auditors are charged with ensuring that the dollars in grants and contracts are spent as intended and that in return for those dollars there is a deliverable. This investment is our tax dollars at work. The dollars come with an expectation of wise management and a return on the investment, whether in technology, a growing business community, advances in science, or education and other programs. Spending money unwisely and/or frivolously on items which do not benefit the purpose of programs or ensure a specific or possible outcome leaves all of us (taxpayers) holding the bag.

All right, you are probably thinking, "Well I wouldn't do that!" You may not. Someone else may. How can the government minimize the chance and know what is going on? Through required information. Through specific recordkeeping and documentation. By monitoring.

For the small business which pursues and receives government funds, either as a grant, contract, or cooperative agreement – whether directly from a government agency or through a prime recipient, the mandatory requirements to capture and provide specific performance data place an additional degree of complexity and capability on what are most often non-existent or weak financial and administrative processes, systems, and control mechanisms.

Because small businesses have limited funds available for any expenditure, they are often reluctant to spend those dollars on administrative systems, including accounting. So how do small businesses implement and maintain financial and managerial control systems which are cost effective and efficient, don't place an undue financial burden or time element on the business, and still have the capability to satisfy the reporting and control requirements?

Step one in the process is to understand the role of financial and managerial controls in robust businesses.

Step two is to understand the requirements being placed on the business related to federal funds.

Step three is to establish policies which address the key operational, financial, and managerial controls in the business.

Step four is to find a system and process which fits the organization.

It is vitally important to understand that for-profit organizations are held to a high level of monitoring and compliance. The "profit" motive of commercial organizations leads government agencies to take steps to ensure grant recipients operate in a manner which is in the best interest of the government and the taxpayers it represents.

Businesses held to these high standards have two challenges. The first is to identify and understand the precise requirements of each grant. The second is to determine the appropriate approach to meet them. This book is intended to provide the basics of what a business must understand about the financial aspects of SBIR awards. It is specifically about the why, what, and how. Understanding these key principles and concepts will enable you to build a sound compliance foundation for your business.

Remember, there is no one-size-fits-all solution. These guidelines and information, however, will enable the design of a solution which fits your particular business needs. Tailoring the solution to your business based upon its specific structure, requirements, and guidelines is necessary to address both the business and compliance needs of the organization. It is a process which begins with the first award – day one, dollar one.

Costs

Actual Costs

The amount incurred, expended, and/or obligated by the recipient which is related to the execution of the project and completion of the scope of work, as well as a share of the common (indirect) costs of the business.

When determining budgets and establishing accounting systems, it is important to remember this: the government is to be charged only the actual cost of an item, whether that is a direct or indirect cost. Although interim or provisional rates for billing purposes are used initially, the actual cost cannot be ignored. The business is responsible for ensuring that only actual costs are ultimately charged to a project. Differences between interim/provisional rates used for billing and the actual costs of those items are to be identified and reported, either at the end of a specific project or annually at fiscal year end. The differences between actual indirect rates and provisional rates, as well as any differences in direct costs, are to be identified and adjustments calculated for over or under charges.

In some instances, maximum indirect rates or other limitations have been placed on specific projects – line items and cost types. In these cases actual costs may not be fully recoverable. Also, the effect of changes in expenditures of line items versus approved budget, mix of direct and indirect costs, and maximum fee amounts are all elements that must be analyzed and accounted for.

Fixed price projects under SBIR policy do not allow for charging more than actual costs to the project. Actual direct and indirect costs are the maximum charge amounts. Further, no fee included in the project may exceed the amount included in the approved budget. The "savings" achieved on any project in direct or indirect costs are not transferable into the fee.

Lea A. Strickland, MBA CMA CFM CBM

Budgeted Costs

The estimated or planned expenditures to be made in executing the scope of work for a project – direct and indirect.

A budget is the "best" estimates of the costs required for a particular project or the business as a whole. It includes required and anticipated business activities during the established budget period – calendar or fiscal year. It is also the value of expenditures expected to be made by the recipient for the execution of the scope of work for a particular project and the business activity which will occur in the same period.

Budgets are important to recipients for the following reasons:

- The "price" of the award is set based upon the agreed upon budget and items included in the budget.
- Any additional funds needed to run the business during a particular period of time are identified.
- The recipient is able to understand how much or how little of total costs of a particular project will be funded by an award.
- The portion or share of indirect costs generated by the business which are not a result of direct activity of a particular project and are recoverable through an award are calculated.

When developing a project budget, it is important to look at the impact on shared business costs as well as those directly related to the project. Every new project impacts all existing projects, planned projects, and the totality of the operations of the business in just about every way. The business must look at the capacity of subject matter experts and technology team members to determine if they can support the level of effort needed. Basics such as office space, computers, and other facilities, as well as specialized research and laboratory equipment may be at or near capacity. Support activities such as program management, accountants, and research assistants may be needed, because all the planned internal projects, commercial clients, and government funded projects combine to consume existing capacity of these resources.

Recipients who look only at each individual project will often miss out on the ability to recover costs associated with the growth of the business, because they fail to identify, quantify, and plan for the necessary expansion of the business infrastructure needed to support multiple projects. If you do not know what your organization will need to look like during the time period when projects are to be performed (and you are an early stage company with plans to grow), then you do not create the opportunity to request the level of indirect costs your business needs to recover the full "share" that can be properly attributed to a project.

When a business invests the time and effort into developing financially sound budgets (how the money will be used in a particular project) and forecasts (how much money will be needed in future periods and how it will be used as an organization) it may enable the business to have a higher proportion of allowable costs to be recovered on each project. Why? How? By having support documentation on assumptions, projections, and future needs identified, a business is able to demonstrate that it is understands its business and the costs associated with it. That understanding enables the business to propose and negotiate reimbursement rates (provisional indirect rates) which more closely align with what is expected than accepting the standard rate offered.

The business which understands the difference between the total cost to the business and the total cost allowed under award terms and conditions is a business prepared to do business.

Guidelines for budgets:

- Proposed hours of work for any employee should not exceed 2080 hours per year
- Proposed salaries are supportable by employment contract, independent salary studies, or other document
- Proposed charges for "direct" employees identify and recognize any portion of activities which may be administrative or unallowable.
- Direct and indirect activities are used to classify costs related to personnel and other costs.
- Consultants are identified separately and used only when essential expertise is not otherwise available.
- Consultant rates are supported by agreements, quotes, or other documents as appropriate to nature and type of services, and the scope of work to be performed.
- Equipment is identified as project specific or general purpose.
- Equipment costs are based on market prices, quotes, or other documentation as appropriate.
- Supplies may be direct or indirect but must be treated consistently regardless of the source of funding.
- Travel costs are based upon government rates for allowability and reasonableness.

Total Costs

As defined by the program, all allowable expenditures which are equitable and consistent in the method determined.

The total costs of a project or award may be different from the viewpoint of the recipient and that of the SBIR awarding agency. The total cost of a particular project for a recipient who has only one project, an SBIR project, underway in its newly formed organization may view all expenditures and costs occurring in the company at that time as part of the "total costs" of the project, but that perspective is not shared under SBIR guidelines and regulations.

Things such as rent, utilities, phones, and administrative expenditures are costs of being in business. The SBIR award covers only that portion of those costs generated by applying the indirect cost rate to the applicable direct cost base.

Example:

Award	$500,000

Company Expenditures During Award Period

Direct Costs	$360,000
Indirect Costs	$140,000
Total	$500,000

Allowable Award Charges

Direct Costs of the project	$360,000
Provisional Indirect Cost Rate 25%	
Indirect Costs Recoverable in Project	$90,000
Total	$450,000

Difference	($50,000)

In this simple example, the recipient must cover $50,000 of indirect expenses from non-award funds.

Let's take this example another step further and add in a 7% fee.

Fee (7% of total allowable costs)	$31,500
Difference	($18,500)

The fee enables the recipient to charge or recover an additional $31,500 of costs for the award period. There remains a need for $18,500 from other funding sources to cover the total costs of the business for the period.

This example, while simple, illustrates the following points:

- Even if the award is the only project going on in the recipient organization at the time of the award, the total expenditures or costs for the recipient in an award period may not be fully recovered.
- The indirect expenditures of the recipient are shared between the project and the business. The project is not viewed as having 100% benefit of the costs of doing business. Because some costs exist whether the project exists or not, the project is allocated only a "fair share" of those business costs.
- The fee in a project may or may not be profit to the bottom-line of the recipient. In fact, more often than not, the fee will be used by the recipient to cover unallowable costs or portions of the indirect costs not recovered under the indirect rate agreement.

From this example, let's move on to discuss the elements of cost.

Lea A. Strickland, MBA CMA CFM CBM

Direct Costs

Those expenditures caused by a specific activity, project, or event which benefit only that activity, project, or event.

Direct costs are a result of an activity, a project, an event…a single cause. The ability to identify the cost with the originating cause – the source – is key to classifying the cost as direct. Direct costs may include: labor, equipment, expendable equipment, supplies, consultants, subawards, subcontracts, and many others.

Many businesses, due to the nature of the technologies and products under development, have projects which consist of activities which may:

- Fall within the scope of multiple projects
- Advance the research and development of multiple projects, products, etc.
- Provide supporting technology to a project
- Provide ancillary products or other inputs used in the project
- Consist of employee time which is not readily segmented into discrete increments that can be attributed to individual projects or technology advances.

Those activities may in fact benefit a single project or they may benefit a group of projects. The single project may be one that has not been defined by the business – an internal research and development platform technology project. It may be that the activity (and its costs) benefits multiple projects because it has been included in multiple projects and has been funded multiple times (a prohibited practice).

Whether a cost is direct – caused by a single activity or benefiting a single project – is based upon an analysis of the underlying documentation, processes, scope of work, acceptable cost practices, and cost principles.

Direct costs are identifiable with a single activity or cause. In cases where a recipient has "direct" expenditures benefiting more than one project funded by one or more government program, the classification of those expenses as "direct" must be carefully analyzed, well-documented, and avoid being charged to multiple projects.

There are occasions when one activity is within the scope of work to be accomplished on two or more projects as proposed – one task/effort with an outcome/result in two or more projects! Use extreme caution in these cases; the same activity cannot be funded by multiple governmental funding sources. It is important to distinguish and document the connection between work and a specific project when dealing with direct charges. A charge cannot be "direct" if the connection and document are not clear and concrete.

Lea A. Strickland, MBA CMA CFM CBM

Among the categories of direct costs, direct labor requires particular care in classification and documentation. (Timekeeping and timesheets are addressed in subsequent sections of this book.) Where the direct labor activities appear to "benefit multiple projects" care must be exercised to:

- Prevent the same activity being funded by multiple governmental projects
- Prevent assignment of costs based upon funding availability
- Ensure that costs are not allocated across projects based on funding, budgets, benefit, or any other basis (indirect costs are allocated, direct costs attach to an activity)
- Protect against shifting of costs between projects or activities.

The practice of apportioning an employee's time across projects which benefit from his/her activity (i.e. an employee works eight hours on a software program and the program will be used on hardware that is used in four projects, so you split the time equally across the four projects) is a method of allocation of shared cost. Shared costs are not direct costs of a project – they are indirect costs (more on this later). This shares the costs due to the availability of funding, and is not based on direct activity or actual relationship between cause and cost. The costs may in fact be direct; direct to a software development project that the company has not defined.

As an example*, let's say you custom manufacture 200 widgets which are the customized proprietary technology of your company. They are to be used across 6 projects. The cost of the 200 widgets is $20,000. You charged each project $3,333.33. You use the widgets in the following quantities:

Project	Quantity Used	Amount Charged	Cost based on Units	Over/ (Under) Charge to Project
A	21	$3,333.33	$2,100	$1,233.33
B	47	$3,333.33	$4,700	($1,366.67)
C	10	$3,333.33	$1,000	$2,333.33
D	11	$3,333.33	$1,100	$2,233.33
E	62	$3,333.33	$6,200	($2,866.67)
F	8	$3,333.33	$800	$2,533.33
"Excess"	41		$4,100	$4,100,00
Total	200	$20,000	$20,000	$0.00*

*Rounding error ignored for purposes of example.

As you can see from the table above, the methods of cost assignment create a substantial difference in the costs of each project. The method of allocating costs based upon the number of projects versus tracking cost based upon the number of units used demonstrates the potential for shifting costs between projects. When expenditures are made that benefit multiple projects, the method used to assign cost must result in a "fair share" being charged to a particular project based upon the benefit received. Specifically identifying the number of units used in each project to accomplish the work makes clear the direct relationship between cost and project.

Undoubtedly you are wondering about the 41 "excess" units in the example. What about those costs? Where will they be charged? Well, the answer depends upon those widgets. Are they still good product – meaning can they still be used in other projects or in actual production? Then they remain on the books as materials or inventory available to use. If they are not usable for future projects, then the costs of those items would be a business expense flowing into indirect costs. If the widget design was created specifically for those six projects, then the total costs per widget could be recalculated ($20,000 divided by 159 widgets). This would proportionately track the direct costs of the total production to the 159 widgets used.

This example illustrates the difference which can result from the method used to track costs to projects. Consistent treatment and methods must be used to ensure that direct costs are charged appropriately to projects and that indirect costs are treated as indirect costs. The objective is to make sure there is no inappropriate shifting of cost between projects.

Direct salaries and wages is another area where the tracking and reporting of time can result in a shift in costs between projects and cost categories (direct, indirect, and unallowable). More on this topic under the time and effort reporting section in later sections of this book.

Indirect Costs

Those costs resulting from projects, activities, processes, or events which benefit a group of projects or the business has a whole. Indirect costs are commonly referred to as overhead, general and administrative, and/or facilities and administrative costs.

Lea A. Strickland, MBA CMA CFM CBM

Overhead Costs

The ongoing expenses of processes and operations which support the organization and are part of producing goods or services, exclude general and administration related costs. These may be associated with a product line, organizational group, or groups of projects, or contracts.

Overhead costs can be summarized as indirect costs related to the performance of a group of projects.

These are some typical overhead costs:

- Supervision of manufacturing or other "production" facilities
- Fringes on overhead labor
- Rent of production facilities
- Cost of utilities and other items traceable to production facilities
- Depreciation costs associated with production facilities

General and Administrative (G&A) or Facilities and Administration (F&A) Costs

Any financial, management, or other costs incurred which relate to the general administration of the business (or business unit) as a whole.

F&A versus G&A: What's the Difference?

The primary difference in the application of these terms to your indirect rate category stems from including or excluding depreciation and use allowances on buildings, equipment and capital improvements, and other related categories of costs. The term "facilities" is generally used to refer to the category of costs associated with the "using up" of tangible personal and real property associated with the business. Some businesses may have depreciation and other use allowance excluded from their cost bases because the resources being used have been funded in total through federal programs. Traditionally, the term facilities and administration (F&A) was used to refer to not-for-profit and governmental recipients cost structures and general and administrative (G&A) terminology was applied to for-profit or commercial entity activities. The term "F&A" has become the standard language used to refer to costs associated with the general activities of the business.

Administration costs are defined as the common costs of being in and running the business, regardless of the types of activities (customers, projects, programs, activities, or processes). These costs exist because the business exists and include the following:

- Accounting
- Administration support
- Personnel/human resources
- Finance
- Professional fees
- Fringe benefits on G&A (F&A) labor
- Office supplies
- Rent on administrative offices
- Utilities associated with administrative offices
- Depreciation on physical assets associated with administrative offices

Fringe Benefits

Fringe benefits are defined as payroll taxes, paid-time-off (holiday, sick, personal, and vacation time), insurance, 401(k) contributions, and any other benefit the business provides its employees. Fringe benefits are commonly treated as indirect costs and pooled for allocation based upon salaries and wages.

Allowable Costs

The expenditures which are authorized based upon the scope of work to be undertaken; the budget as submitted, negotiated, and approved; which are necessary and reasonable for the type of recipient and activities engaged in; are consistent in treatment (direct and indirect) across projects and periods regardless of funding source; are not expressly prohibited by regulations, policy, agency, legislation, program, or terms/conditions of award agreement; and are adequately documented.

Lea A. Strickland, MBA CMA CFM CBM

Four Point Test

Determining whether or not a cost is allowable can be accomplished using what is commonly referred to as "the four point test":

1. Is the cost reasonable?
   a. Nature and type of activity
   b. Nature and type of business
   c. Customary price or cost for a competitive business
   d. Arms' length or negotiated price
   e. Whether or not a "prudent" business person would make this type of expenditure
2. Is the cost allocable to the project?
3. Is the treatment/classification of the cost consistent with how similar costs are treated?
4. Is the cost in conformance with cost standards and accounting principles?

To answer these questions you must first understand each of the concepts or principles underlying the questions.

Reasonable

A cost which by its nature and amount does not exceed the cost a prudent person would incur in the running of a competitive business.

The following questions are generally accepted as the checkpoints for the reasonableness of a cost:

- Is the cost one generally considered to be necessary to the operations of the business or the project?
- Does the cost comply with the company's own standards and policies?
- Was the expenditure of the cost in keeping with the amount and nature of "due prudence"?

Allocable

> A cost assignable or chargeable to one or more cost objectives on the basis of proportion of benefits received or another equitable relationship.

Costs are allocable to a government project if they are incurred specifically for that project; they are direct costs. Costs may also be allocated to a government project if the project receives benefit from the activity as long as the allocation of such costs is based upon a reasonable proportional relationship or the costs are necessary to keep the business operational. Costs allocated based upon benefit are indirect costs.

The method of allocation must be such that it does not result in cost shifting (a disproportionate amount of costs being charged to a single government project or government projects as a group). Allocation on the basis of availability of funds on a particular government project is not a reasonable basis, even if the project budget included amounts for indirect costs.

Allocation methods are to be documented (cost allocation plans) and remain consistent across projects and reporting periods. Changes in allocation methods should be annotated on financial statements used in reporting and as support for calculation of rates or financial performance.

Consistency

The nature of the cost incurred results from acceptable methods and practices under Cost Accounting Standards Board guidelines and/or Generally Accepted Accounting Principles and must be applied in the same way under similar circumstances.

While a cost may be charged either as direct or indirect, depending upon the identifiable benefit to a particular program, the method of charging costs must be consistent under similar circumstances, regardless of the source of funding. A business may opt to treat a direct cost as indirect where the cost of tracking or administration of the direct cost exceeds the benefit to be derived from treatment as a direct cost. In those cases, all similar costs must also be treated consistently – as indirect costs.

Lea A. Strickland, MBA CMA CFM CBM

Necessary

A cost is necessary when not incurring the expenditure will prevent the business from fulfilling its obligations under contractual obligations to customers, owners, vendors, employees, etc.; maintaining its normal operations and activities; is part of sound business practice which includes arms-length negotiation/pricing, following Federal and State laws and regulations; and is not a significant deviation from established business practices (past performance and policy).

Costs are necessary when the expenditure is part of normal business expenses for a business of that type, stage, industry, and under acceptable processes, practices, and management methods.

Many factors come into play in determining "necessity". A cost which may be viewed as necessary for one type of business, may not be for another. In addition, a cost is not a "necessity" when the cost is incurred due to inadequate management, failure of business systems, or other negligent or poor operating practices.

Unallowable Costs

The expenditures which are expressly excluded from being charged to a project under policy, program directive, legislation, regulation, or the terms and/or conditions of the award agreement.

Unallowable costs are those which are expressly prohibited by policy, program language, regulation, and/or terms of award. For commercial (for-profit) recipients, the allowability of costs guidance comes primarily from the Federal Acquisition Regulation Part 31.2. Each agency generally has its own guidance and policy based upon this regulation, but the tenets are the same.

A cost is unallowable if it fails to meet these requirements:

1. reasonableness
2. allocability
3. cost standards (Cost Accounting Standards Board, Generally Accepted Accounting Principles, and practices related to industry)
4. terms of the agreement
5. limitations as set forth in FAR 31.2

From FAR 31.205 here are some costs that are specifically addressed as either unallowable or unallowable unless certain special conditions are met:

Unallowable:

- Advertising (includes marketing, public relations, etc.)
- Alcoholic beverages
- Bad debt expense
- Contingencies
- Contributions or donations
- Entertainment
- Key life insurance
- Interest and other financial costs of funding
- Lobbying
- Organization costs
- Taxes
- Travel cost in excess of federally allowed amounts

Unallowable unless specified condition is met

- Fines and Penalties - allowable if incurred to comply with specific terms and conditions of the contract
- Independent Research and Development Costs - sponsored by or required in the performance of contract or grant.
- Patent Costs - required by the terms of the Government contract or grant.

Questioned Costs

The expenditures which are reviewed to determine if allowable under the award and are found to lack adequate documentation; appear to be inconsistently applied or categorized for cost type (direct/indirect); or appear to be unreasonable, unnecessary, or unallocable to a project.

A cost may be direct or indirect; reasonable, necessary, allocable, and allowable, but without supporting documentation to verify the validity of the cost in amount, timing, purpose, and related information then, under review or audit, the cost may be questioned. Questioned costs are those which, for whatever reason – amount, timing, type, nature – catch the interest of the program office, the payments division, an indirect cost or other type of auditor.

The question may be as simple as asking for the documentation which supports the transaction and demonstrates that it is within the scope of work and budget as approved. It also may not be that simple.

A cost not supported by documents may be reduced, disallowed, or otherwise acted upon – like triggering an expanded audit of the recipient's total activity and business. When you charge an item to a project – directly or indirectly - you must have supporting documentation. The types and nature of documentation vary with the nature of the transaction.

The following list will give you some ideas of the documents needed:

Equipment purchase (item $5,000 or more and with a life of 1 year or more)	■ Technical specifications ■ Quotes ■ Purchase order ■ Invoice ■ Payment record – check, funds transfer, etc. ■ Title ■ Shipping documents ■ Asset list
Supplies	■ Receipt ■ Expense report
Travel Expenses - airfare	■ Boarding passes ■ Itinerary ■ Expense report ■ Credit card statement ■ Payment verification
Salaries and wages (More on this under the time and effort section of this book)	■ Properly executed timesheet ■ Project lists ■ Policy and definitions of how time is to be charged ■ Activities

More on recordkeeping and documentation requirements in the recordkeeping section of this book.

Disallowed Costs

The expenditures made and charged to a particular award or group of awards for activities which are not allowed; for items treated inconsistently; for amounts which are excessive, unreasonable, or unnecessary; or for items which lack documentation or are inadequately documented.

Disallowed costs result from the review of costs which have been charged to an award and are determined to be inappropriate. The disallowed cost may be direct or indirect in nature. Amounts disallowed may be the full amount or some portion of the amount charged, depending upon the item, nature of charges, and the defect in the transaction or recordkeeping.

Disallowed costs may also be costs which are normally considered "allowable" under terms, conditions, and other policies or guidance. These expenditures become disallowed when any of the following occurs:

- No supporting documentation – for instance no timesheets
- Inadequate support documentation – time sheets which are not properly executed, items purchased but which have no receipts or invoices
- Inconsistent treatment – direct travel costs charged to government projects but not tracked and charged to commercial customer projects
- Unreasonable amounts – the purchase of services from a less qualified consultant at a higher rate than could have been obtained from a more qualified consultant
- Unnecessary – the expenditure was outside the scope of activity/work called for in the project
- Defective allocation method – the basis for sharing indirect costs between projects and activities resulted in a shift of costs to the government funded project and away from internal and commercial customer projects.

Fees

An amount charged to a project in addition to the direct and indirect costs. Many agencies, programs, or projects will have established maximum rates.

Fee requests are to be based upon a logical and/or justifiable basis, such as margins consistent with all other projects of similar scope. Requested fees are not necessarily going to be awarded in full. The typical fee is around 7% - some higher, some lower.

While fees are to be set based upon customary profit levels, the actual amount received may or may not equate to profits for the business. There are two primary reasons for the difference between fees and profit: (1) unallowable costs, and (2) differences between actual indirect rates and final indirect rates. In some cases ceilings (limits on) the final indirect rates prevent recovery of the total indirect costs allocable to a project. In others, the business has substantial unallowable costs. In both these instances and others which are similar, the fee will, in effect, be the means for covering costs not recoverable as a part of project costs.

Accounting

System Requirements

The processes, controls, and other mechanisms used to identify, track, monitor, control, and report on the financial performance of the company, its projects and activities.

Where is the best starting place when talking about an accounting system, what comprises a system, and what it must do? It is probably best to begin by understanding that the government does not dictate the accounting system. It may be manual or automated, cash or accrual based. The government does specify what results the system must be capable of generating.

The accounting system must meet the requirements for:

- internal controls
- properly identifying costs by project/program
- segregating costs by type
- generating reports by project/program and total
- separating job responsibilities, roles, and duties to maintain adequate controls over
  - cash receipts and disbursements
  - verification of accounts payable and receipts
  - recording transactions
  - changes made
  - authorization of changes, journal entries

The accounting system must also include the following:

- chart of accounts
- financial reports by project and in total
- adequate supporting documentation
- ability to generate invoices and payments
- ability to track and report cash balances and government funds on hand accurately
- ability to identify, segregate, and report program income
- ability to identify, calculate, report and remit interest earned on government funds
- ability to track, segregate, and report assets acquired with federal funds
- ability to differentiate individual transactions such as receipt of funds and use of those funds

Cash or Accrual Based Transactions

In the event that a program or agency specifies that all reports are to be on an accrual-basis, the recipient is not required to change from cash to accrual basis, but must be capable of generating the reports under accrual accounting methods. Often the accounting software used provides this option as part of its report generation capability. In order for this option to work, the business must be entering transactions in a manner which supports conversion of transactions.

For instance, vendor invoices and other bills would be entered at time received. Under cash based accounting, the invoice would not be recognized as part of expenses until paid. Under the accrual method, the invoice would be included in expenses at the time it is received and entered.

The accounting system must be able to identify transactions made by project, activity, cost type, and cost pool as appropriate. This may be accomplished within the actual accounting software package or through "add-ons" utilizing spreadsheet or other "manual" processes. As long as the business is capable of producing the information AND it reconciles in total back to the accounting records, then the "system" is acceptable.

From an execution standpoint, this means that each transaction (recording, reviewing, or reporting) must be captured as part of the financial activity of the business and at an activity or project level. Both direct costs and indirect costs must be captured accurately. Each, however, is treated differently. Capturing direct costs is relatively straightforward: each transaction is documented to show direct costs are clearly tracked and reported against the project which causes them.

Capturing indirect costs requires that all indirect costs of the business are pooled into specific accounts and groups of accounts. Those costs are subsequently allocated to projects on the appropriate cost bases. This facilitates the calculation of the actual indirect costs during the fiscal and reporting periods.

Costs which are expressly unallowable or have been excluded upon agreement are to be identified and excluded from billing, claim, and proposals. These costs are not included in direct or indirect charges to a project but remain part of the total costs of doing business for the recipient. Unallowable costs must be covered from non-federal funding sources or from the fee paid for various projects. Unallowable costs incurred under a project as direct expenses cannot be shifted to indirect cost pools for allocation and recovery.

Whether your accounting system is manual (spreadsheets and paper records or inexpensive pre-packaged software and paper files) or automated (transactions are recorded and generated within an enterprise-wide system – everything from purchase orders to checks are generated within the accounting system) no system stands without written policies and procedures. In order to demonstrate that the business has a robust financial management and control system, the why, how, who, and when of doing business and accounting for those activities must be specified in writing to demonstrate and have a robust financial management and control system.

Chart of Accounts

The account structure established in the accounting system to identify costs by meaningful category for financial, tax, and/or managerial accounting purposes. These are the major categories of accounts:

Assets

Liabilities

Owner/Shareholder Equity

The major account categories are subdivided into more discrete accounts. A basic chart of account structure typically includes the following:

- Current Assets
    - Cash
    - Accounts receivable
    - Inventory
    - Prepayments/deposits

- Property Plant and Equipment/Fixed Assets
    - Equipment – Lab
    - Accumulated depreciation – Lab Equipment
    - Equipment – Office
    - Accumulated depreciation – Office
    - Leasehold improvements
    - Accumulated depreciation – Leasehold

- Other Assets
    - Patents
    - Amortization – Patents

- Current Liabilities
- Long Term Liabilities
- Equity

Revenue

- Direct Program Expenses
    - Direct salaries and wages
    - Consultants
    - Equipment
    - Materials and supplies
    - Travel
    - Consortium costs
- Fringe benefits
    - Vacation
    - Holidays
    - Sick leave
    - Payroll taxes
    - Retirement/401(k)
    - Group insurance

- Indirect Expenses
  - Overhead
    - Labor (Salaries and Wages)
    - Depreciation
    - Amortization
    - Rent
    - Utilities
    - Telephone
    - Equipment rentals
    - Expendable equipment
    - General lab supplies
    - Travel
    - Consultants
  - General and Administrative
    - Labor (Salaries and Wages)
    - Amortization
    - Depreciation
    - Rent
    - Utilities
    - Telephone
    - Equipment rental
    - Expendable equipment
    - Office supplies
    - Travel
    - Consultants
    - Legal – Corporate/General
    - Accounting
    - Insurance
    - Licenses
    - Dues and subscriptions
    - Postage

- Internal/Independent Research and Development
  - Labor (salaries and wages)

- Unallowables
  - Interest expense
  - Advertising
  - Alcoholic beverages
  - Entertainment
  - Contributions

Segregation of costs

The ability to identify costs by type (direct, indirect, overhead, general and administrative, and unallowable) and associate each of those items with the project, activity, or segment of the business – a basic requirement for federal fund recipients. The segregation of costs into meaningful financial reports facilitates the reporting by project, as well as the allocation of shared costs based upon benefit.

The accounting system established must be able to track direct costs, provide a mechanism for pooling common costs, and support the selection and calculation of the basis of allocation.

Program Income

Program income is income generated directly by the grant-supported project or activity or earned as a result of the award during the grant period. It may include but is not limited to the following:

- Income from fees for services performed
- Use or rental of real or personal property acquired under federally-funded projects
- Sale of commodities or items fabricated under an award
- License fees and royalties on patents and copyrights
- Interest on loans made with award funds

What is NOT program income?

- Interest earned on advances of Federal funds
- Receipt of principal on loans
- Rebates
- Credits
- Discounts
- Interest earned on any of the above items

Recipients are expected to have a written policy which defines program income and details how the company identifies and tracks program income. The policy should detail specific recordkeeping requirements and procedures for ensuring that all program income is identified, segregated, accounted for, and handled per the terms and conditions of each project and/or award. The policy should also identify who in the organization is responsible for program income related activity and recordkeeping.

Program income requires that accounting and management control systems be capable of reporting by program, project, source, as well as the remittance or use of program income under the terms and conditions of each award instrument.

Program income is retained by the grantee and is used subject to the terms and conditions specified by the program and/or agency. These are options for dealing with program income:

- Additive alternative – added to the funds committed to the project to further eligible objectives

- Deductive alternative – deducted from total project or program allowable costs in determining the net allowable costs on which the Federal share of costs will be based
- Matching alternative – used to satisfy all or part of the non-Federal share of a project or program
- Combination alternative –use all program income up to (and including) a specified amount as additive alternative and any amount of program income exceeding the specified amount as under the deductive alternative

Indirect
Cost
Rates

Indirect Cost Rates

Indirect cost rates are used to determine fairly and conveniently, keeping in mind cost principles, what portion of indirect costs will be associated with each program or project. The indirect cost rate is the ratio between the total allowable indirect expenses and the designated direct cost base (See Direct Cost Base section of this book). Indirect cost rates may be calculated using a simplified (single rate) method or a multiple rate method, which is more common for commercial entities.

Simplified Method – Single Rate

A single indirect cost rate consolidates and allocates (apportions) all indirect costs, utilizing the same direct cost base.

Multiple Rate Method – Two- and Three-Tier Systems

A two-tier indirect cost system usually consists of a fringe costs rate and an indirect rate (overhead and facilities/general and administrative rates). The two rates may be applied on different direct cost bases.

A three-tier indirect cost system is comprised of a fringe rate, overhead rate, and a rate which may be referred to as general and administrative (G&A) or facilities and administrative (F&A) rate. Again, each rate may be applied on a different cost base.

Indirect Cost Rate Calculations

To calculate indirect cost rate(s), follow these steps:

- select a one, two, or three tier indirect rate structure
- segregate costs by type: direct and indirect (fringe, overhead, and F&A (G&A)) costs, as well as the identification of unallowable expenses or excluded expenses (for example on subcontract costs – the amount in excess of $25,000 that may be excluded from the direct cost base)
- identify the appropriate direct cost base
- perform the calculations

Direct Cost Base

The direct cost base is the allocation basis used to apportion costs between programs, projects, or funding sources. The direct cost base may consist of the following:

- Direct salaries and wages
- Total direct costs
- Modified total direct costs

Selecting an appropriate direct cost base is important to the organization. This is how it "recovers" a fair proportion of the shared or common costs from a specific project. The objective in selecting the direct cost base is to identify which option most accurately reflects the relationship of indirect costs to direct activities. The relationship between direct and indirect costs can differ significantly for each organization. One business' cost structure may be weighted toward direct salaries and wages – the labor activity. Another business may find that, due to automation of research processes, labor expenses are a smaller proportion of costs, and machine hours is a more appropriate allocation base. Another may have more expendable and capital equipment in its cost structure.

It is important for each organization to understand its own cost structure – the relationship between direct and indirect costs – AND understand the direct cost base options available. Understanding the cost and activity relationship enables the business to develop the best indirect cost rate structure for its particular operations. It also enables the business to manage project and business costs more effectively.

It is also important to note that comparing indirect cost rates between organizations can be misleading. Difference in cost structures, activities, types of businesses, and the items included or excluded from the cost base do not facilitate meaningful comparisons.

Let's review each direct cost base alternative.

Direct Salaries and Wages

The first direct cost base option uses direct salaries and wages. This category of cost base can be calculated in two different ways. Determining which option to use depends upon the cost treatment and practices (conformity, consistency…) selected by the business in accounting for these costs.

Direct salaries and wages are the compensation amounts of each employee – the pay rates. During the budget phase, the direct salaries and wages are the planned pay rates. These may be based upon a set hourly wage or an annual salary amount established for a standard work schedule (i.e. 40 hour weeks, 2080 hours per year; 12 months; or other customary increment of time relevant to the business' operational plan). Direct salaries and wages may include or exclude fringe benefits – again depending upon how the business has decided to treat costs.

The business may choose to include fringe benefits as part of the salaries and wages as direct costs or may choose to total all fringe benefits together and allocate them on the basis of salaries and wages to the various activities and programs. Due to the consistency requirement, in whatever manner the business decides to handle these costs, it must continue to do so for all projects – governmental, internal, and external (commercial) – and across all time periods (year to year, project to project, etc.).

Total Direct Costs

Total direct costs are the most inclusive of the cost bases. This base includes direct salaries and wages, as well as "other" direct costs. This cost base includes these items:

- Direct salaries and wages
- Fringe benefits associated with direct salaries and wages
- Direct materials and supplies
- Direct services
- Direct travel
- Subcontracts up to $25,000 each

Modified Total Direct Costs

As the name implies, modified total direct costs begin with the total direct costs and is then modified to exclude certain items of expense. This cost base excludes from the total direct cost base equipment and subcontract amounts over $25,000.

Allocation Base Impact

Because the allocation base is meant to provide an "equitable" distribution of indirect costs, a cost base may be adjusted to ensure that a fair distribution of expenses occurs.

Types of Indirect Cost Rates

Just as there are various methods of calculating indirect rates, there are multiple types of indirect cost rates. The type of rate to be calculated depends upon the stage of business, program, and project. Here are the various categories of rates:

- provisional
    - temporary "billing"
    - negotiated
- final
- ceiling or cap
- pre-determined
- fixed

Provisional Rate

A provisional rate is just that – an interim rate established until the actual indirect costs can be determined and a final rate is established. It is used both for budgeting and payment of funds. A provisional rate may be a "temporary billing rate" used pending the negotiation of the awardee's rate or the "negotiated rate" resulting from a reviewed and accepted indirect cost proposal.

Final Rate

The final rate is established after the business knows the actual costs for a given accounting period, usually the fiscal year. The final indirect rate is used to adjust the indirect costs claimed in the award proposal, budget, and payments. The adjustment is the difference between the actual rate and the provisional rate up to any ceiling amount.

Ceiling or Cap Rate

The ceiling or cap rate is the maximum amount of indirect costs which can be charged to a particular project (fixed dollar amount or fixed percentage). This ceiling rate may be set by the originating program authorization legislation, through negotiated agreement (acceptance of award terms), or through limitation of costs/funds clauses.

Pre-determined Rate

The pre-determined rate is a permanent rate established for a specified period (current or future) and cannot be changed or adjusted after the fact. The rate is typically used on awards where costs to be incurred are reasonably assured and not likely to exceed the organization's actual costs.

Fixed Rate

A fixed rate is a permanent rate. It has the same characteristics of the pre-determined rate but allows for differences between actual and estimated costs to be "carried forward" to future periods. The fixed rate is subject to adjustment based upon actual costs. Such adjustments are applied to future periods of performance (usually fiscal year).

Organization Impact of Different Types of Rates

Most businesses, especially those early stage companies which are still establishing their business infrastructure and operations, prefer an uncapped or no ceiling provisional rate for the following reasons:

- the cost structure of the business is uncertain
- the ability to forecast future periods when actual project performance will occur is dependent upon operational assumptions which may change significantly as the business evolves
- prior year financial results may not reflect future operational structures and activities
- provisional rates without ceilings allow "adjustments" and recovery of actual costs incurred
- the project costs, as well as the business costs, are identifiable (because this is a requirement of cost reimbursement awards) and enable the business to understand cost structures that result from specific activities and projects

A well-constructed indirect cost rate proposal makes the difference in what rate is awarded. A proposal that is based upon well-documented assumptions and includes a "roll-up" of costs based on actual or planned rates, hours, and other support documentation, enables the business to demonstrate its understanding of financial management and costs. A poorly prepared proposal damages the credibility of the recipient's financial management system and undermines its ability to obtain rates above the "standard".

Indirect Cost Proposals

An indirect cost proposal (ICP) is based upon the applicable cost principle (FAR 31); the cost policy, practices, and methods of the business; and the anticipated costs and cost structure of a particular project and the business in total. It is documentation of the calculation, assumptions, and analysis of the expected indirect cost rate or rates the business expects during the performance of a project.

The indirect cost proposal is submitted to the oversight or cognizant cost group for the awarding agency or, in the case of a recipient with multiple awards and awarding agencies, – the agency with the largest proportion of total dollars awarded. The indirect cost proposal includes this information:

- historic financials
  - most recent completed fiscal year financial statements
  - year-to-date financial statements
- projected or forecasted financial statements
  - emainder of current fiscal year statement
  - next fiscal year financial statement
- fiscal year(s) of project period
- segregated cost analysis (financials divided by direct, indirect, unallowable, by project, IR&D, etc.)
- budget for project
- calculation of cost bases
- calculation of indirect rates

Indirect Cost Negotiation

It is unusual for an indirect cost negotiation to be required unless the proposed rate exceeds the specified allowable rate for each phase of the SBIR program. In Phase I, that would be 40% of total direct costs; in Phase II, 25% of total direct costs. If a project proposal does not include a proposed rate over these guidelines, then an indirect cost proposal will not be required. If the business does request a rate based upon total direct costs which is above these rates, then the program office will notify the agency's indirect cost group – the group representing the agency with the largest dollar award(s) – and request that an indirect cost negotiation be started.

Indirect cost negotiations consist of three stages:

- pre-negotiation
- negotiation
- post-negotiation

In simplest terms, pre-negotiation is the period where the business gathers and reviews facts and figures, identifies issues, and determines the best methods of allocation and cost categorization. The business is engaged in developing its costs and position on what rates will be proposed.

The second stage is the actual negotiation. The indirect cost group will send a letter to the business outlining the negotiation process, the required documents, and the timing for the negotiation. A recipient does not submit indirect cost proposals prior to the receipt of this letter.

The requirement to negotiate indirect rates is usually included in the notice of award and may also specify a timeframe (within 30 – 90 days) within which the recipient must commence the negotiation process. Recipients are expected to communicate with the program office and the designated cost group to ensure that all requirements, processes, and timing are understood and underway.

For recipients who fail to undertake indirect cost negotiations in a timely manner (or at all), the amount of indirect costs allowed may be limited, or eliminated entirely from the project expenditures. The notice of award may actually contain language which limits the amount to be charged to the project prior to obtaining a negotiated rate agreement.

Preparedness and strategy are both important to the negotiation phase. Understanding the process and the ability to develop robust numbers to use during negotiation is critical to the organization's success. The negotiated rates and the cost basis determine how much money can be charged.

The negotiation process may vary from agency to agency; each group, however, is accountable to ensure that the indirect cost rate proposals are

- complete in form and content
- include the nature of the organization
- review the adequacy of financial systems
- review the types of costs included to determine allowability and proper charging of costs
- assess the fairness of cost bases used to make allocations

Lea A. Strickland, MBA CMA CFM CBM

Common Review Questions

Preliminary Review

- Is the business eligible to participate in the program and/or project?
- Are indirect costs being recovered on existing projects or are projects being sought which include indirect cost recovery?
- Is this the first rate negotiation for the organization?
- Are there multiple federal agencies making awards which may require indirect rate negotiations?
- Is the business able to provide all necessary supporting data and documents?
    - Most recent audited or unaudited financial statements
    - Total direct costs incurred or projected under awards
    - Salaries and wages
    - Fringe benefit details
    - Organizational charts
    - Chart of accounts
    - Other related documents
- Is the budget properly prepared?
- Is the business financially capable of performing on its actual and planned awards?
- Is the business "affiliated" with other organizations – venture capital, institutional investors, stockholders, etc.?
- Are there any prior approvals required for special conditions or circumstances?
- Has the organization previously complied with all agreements?
- What audits (federal and non-federal) has the business had?
- What level of effort is needed for the review of the business and audit of submissions?

Cost Allowability

- How do proposed cost compare to historical costs?
- Are the costs proposed consistent with the nature of the scope of work, project type, and business?
- Do the costs included benefit multiple projects – federal and non-federal?
- Are the items included in the cost pools appropriate?
- Are unallowable costs properly identified and excluded?
- Are there costs included that are susceptible to mischarging and if so, how are these costs identified?
- Are costs included handled consistently?

Allocation Bases

- Are the allocation bases used appropriate to the type of activities and costs?
- Do the allocation bases provide an equitable distribution of indirect costs?
- Do the proposed bases include all activities – allowable and unallowable - to ensure that all projects receive a fair share of costs?
- How current are the allocation bases?

General

- Are the mathematical calculations accurate?
- Are there planned or anticipated changes in the operations of the business that are not incorporated into the proposal?
- Which type of rate (provisional, fixed, predetermined) should be used?

Helpful Hints

- The company negotiator should understand the proposal, the process used to prepare the proposal, the cost structure and operations of the business, and the terminology, process, procedures, and other aspects of the type of awards and rates.
- Be prepared for follow up questions
- Invest the time in preparing a complete and reasoned analysis prior to the submission
- Develop and propose costs and rates for multiple years based upon robust forecasts and assumptions

Here is an example:

"indirect costs will be limited to 10% of direct salaries and wages excluding fringe"

Direct salaries and wages	$50,000
Direct fringe benefits	$15,000
Indirect costs (actual)	$50,000

Indirect Cost "Recovery"

Indirect cost provisional rate – 40% of Direct Salaries and fringe ($65,000 X 0.4)	$26,000
Capped indirect rate – 10% of Direct Salaries excluding fringe ($50,000 X 0.1)	$5.000
Impact of indirect rate difference	($21,000)

In some instances, an awarding agency may allow "retroactive" recovery. This means the company may go back to the beginning of the project period and calculate the difference between the temporary provisional rate (10% of Direct Salary without fringe) and the negotiated provisional rate (40% of direct salary with fringe). In other instances, the awarding agency may make the rate effective from the date of negotiation and the cost differential will remain unrecovered.

Indirect Cost Negotiated Agreement

The approved negotiated indirect cost agreement is issued by the authorized representative of the awarding agency's indirect cost group. This document (usually a letter) includes the following information:

- approved rate and information directly related to the use of the rate
    - type of rate
    - effective period
    - direct allocation base
- fringe benefits cost treatment – direct or indirect – and any approved fringe benefit rate
- general terms and conditions
- special remarks or comments on the composition of indirect cost pools, etc.

The negotiated indirect rate agreement letter applies to current awards and future proposals. The negotiated rate prepared and submitted under applicable cost principles and guidelines will usually be accepted by other agencies.

Actual Indirect Cost Submission

The actual costs incurred and the indirect rates which result for a specified period (usually a fiscal year) are submitted annually to the oversight or cognizant cost group. Following review of the actual costs incurred and the resulting rates calculated, a letter similar to that of the negotiated rate agreement is provided to the business. The letter accepting actual rates for the relevant time period states that for projects performed in that timeframe the indirect costs were performed at an indirect rate of x%. The differential between the provisional rate and the actual (final) rate for the period is generally recoverable (subject to ceilings and caps, terms and conditions) from awarding agencies. The determination of final cost letter is sent with a cover letter to each awarding agency/program office with a calculation of the difference between invoiced and actual costs. Each agency/program will review and determine if the adjustment is reimbursable.

It is important to understand that only actual costs can be charged to any program or project. Thus, when actual costs are calculated, if the resulting rates are less than those charged using the provisional rate, then a downward adjustment – repayment to the government – is required.

Reimbursement of Indirect Costs

The adjustments (up or down) between provisional and final rates are always subject to availability of funds, statutory and administrative restrictions (ceilings), approval of the program office, and the administrative and financial requirements, such as documentation, recordkeeping, and allowability tests, for example.   Supplementary items such as program income, cost match/share, and additional terms and conditions will also determine whether or not costs are reimbursable.

General Guidance for Preparing Indirect Cost Rate Proposals

Preparing an indirect cost proposal is a critical step in establishing not only appropriate rates but also the credibility of your organization's ability to manage a project, which includes meeting the administrative and financial systems requirements. A well-prepared proposal is based upon the following process/steps:

1. Know your business
   a. Organizational structure, including organizational charts (formal or informal)
   b. Cost and financial principles
   c. Terms and conditions
   d. Operational and financial policies

   Which groups and activities are:

   - Direct
   - Government projects
     - Internal research and development
     - Commercial client project
   - Indirect
   - Overhead
   - Facilities
   - General and administrative
   - Sales and marketing
   - Raising capital/funding
   - Unallowable
     - Activity
     - Cost

2. Develop a summary of all funding and projects, including restrictions on funds, allowable and unallowable activities, approved rates and cost bases, and differentiate between
   a. Federal
   b. Non-federal
3. Review the accounting structure
   a. Chart of accounts
   b. Segregation of costs by project, cost pool, cost type, etc.
   c. Organizational/operational structure versus accounting structure
4. Prepare written cost policy – how different activities and costs are categorized (direct, indirect, unallowable) and cost base used for allocation of indirect costs
5. Prepare the indirect cost proposal
   a. Separate costs:
      i. direct, indirect, and unallowable
      ii. internal research and development
      iii. commercial
      iv. governmental by program
   b. Organizational structure – chart
   c. Level of Federal Funding
      i. By agency
      ii. By program
   d. Financial reports
   e. Allocation bases
   f. Systems in changes to meet requirements
   g. Calculate bases and indirect rates – historical
   h. Reconcile financial statements (audited or unaudited fiscal period versus structure used for rate calculation
   i. Develop forecast for future performance period
   j. Calculate bases and indirect rates – provisional
   k. Compile documentation to provide support
6. Submit indirect cost proposal to oversight or cognizant agency
7. Respond to agency questions
8. Receive executed rate agreement
9. Apply to awards

Audits

Recipients of federal funds who receive and expend more than $500,000 in a year are required to have a non-governmental audit. Arranging for an audit is the responsibility of the recipient of these federal funds. The recipient is also responsible for completing the appropriate reports and follow-up on audit issues, comments, and findings.

The key to deciding whether or not you meet or exceed the mandatory audit threshold is the ability to determine when an expenditure is made. An expenditure occurs when the activity relates to the execution of the programmatic, administrative, or financial aspects of the project.

The audit is subject to audit requirements for a non-Federal audit. The recipient has two options regarding the type of audit which will satisfy the audit requirements:

- a financial related audit that meets Government Auditing Standards, or
- an audit that meets the requirements contained in OMB Circular No. A-133

The audit period for a financial audit is the fiscal year.

Audits are required for each year the audit threshold is met or exceeded. If the audit threshold is not met, then the business must maintain all records of activities, expenditures, receipts, and transactions which occurred for at least three years after the close out of each award. Documents related to each award and total business activity should be maintained and be available for review or audit by federal government auditors.

All audits are to be completed and submitted to the oversight or cognizant audit office. This must be done prior to the earlier of two dates: (1) 30 days after receipt of the auditor's report(s), or (2) nine months after the end of the audit period (recipient's fiscal year). Note: A company generally has six months from the end of the fiscal year to submit final costs and rates to its oversight or cognizant agency for review and determination.

The audit threshold calculation includes both prime and sub-awards which are flow-throughs from federal awards. The threshold generally excludes fixed price awards.

It is the recipient's responsibility to determine the correct audit agency and file the appropriate documents related to the audit with that agency.

Audit costs are allowable and should be included in the indirect cost structure of the company.

Annual audit reports are to be submitted within 30 days of the receipt of the audit report by the company or nine months after the end of the fiscal year, whichever is earlier. The audit report is submitted to the designated audit clearinghouse or appropriate oversight office of the oversight or cognizant agency. Note once again, due to the requirement to have the final indirect cost proposal within six months of the end of the company's fiscal year, the effective audit completion date is 30 days after receipt of the report or six months from the end of the fiscal year end.

Clarification – audit requirement

In some cases a recipient organization may not meet the audit threshold for conducting a non-governmental audit. This does not mean, however, that a governmental audit will not occur. Governmental audits may be conducted on any SBIR recipient, regardless of the Phase (I or II), amount, or stage of award. The scope and nature of the audit may vary, but falling below the audit threshold simply means you are not required to hire an auditor to review your financial records.

Lea A. Strickland, MBA CMA CFM CBM

Audit Costs

Audit costs are allowable costs when they meet these criteria:

- the selection of the auditor follows objective standards
- the audit being conducted is executed under sound audit principles and practices
- the cost of the audit is reasonable and necessary given the nature and scope of the audit.

Audit costs are usually included in the indirect costs of the business. When budgeting the cost of an audit, the business should consider the following elements:

- salaries, wages, and fees associated with employees, contractors, and consultants involved in the accounting, financial, tax and other aspects of the business
- the fee charged by the audit firm.

The award recipient is responsible for the costs of non-governmental audits. For governmental audits, the recipient is responsible for the costs associated with the company's activities in interacting with and responding to the government auditor. These costs are those associated with the salaries, wages, fees, and other costs of employee time, advisors, consultants, tax advisors, and, if necessary, advice or services from legal advisors.

Governmental Audits

Federal audits conducted by employees or representatives of the government to review financial, operational, and other systems to determine degree of compliance with applicable rules, regulations, terms, and conditions imposed by law or agreement.

It is important for businesses to understand that federal funding comes with expectations and requirements of the nature, scope, activities, administration, and financial performance of projects. To ensure these expectations and requirement are being met, the federal government conducts periodic audits. The purpose of these audits is to monitor compliance – adherence to the requirements specified by law, regulations, policy, and terms and conditions agreed to at some point during the project. In addition, an audit will identify exceptions, issues, and possible risks as a result of changing conditions

When a company submits a proposal for federal assistance (grant, cooperative agreement, contract, or other instrument), that entity makes these statements:

- they meet the qualifications for participating in the program at the time of proposal
- they accept the terms, conditions, and other restrictions placed on the use of funds, operations, and activities of the organization
- they are willing to put in place financial control and business management systems or modify existing systems to become capable of complying with all aspects of requirements associated with the funding received
- they are or will become capable by the time of award – technologically, administratively, and financially.

Governmental audits may occur at any time regarding many areas of the award. Particular emphasis is given to the following areas:

- program eligibility
- financial capability
- business management systems and controls
- financial results and activities
- taxes
- Department of Labor compliance
- Other areas

It is the company's responsibility to know and understand the full range of regulatory compliance for an organization in its industry, of its size, and type of activity. The organization is expected to be in compliance with all applicable state and federal laws and with the terms and conditions of the specific agreements it has entered into.

Cost of Governmental Audits

The cost of the government's auditors is not charged to the audited company. However, any costs that the company must incur for employees, consultants, contractors, legal advisors, or tax advisors related to the company's activities and support of the government's audit activity is the expense of the auditee.

The costs of audits, federal and non-federal, are normally allowable as indirect costs of the organization.

Non-governmental Audits

Audits conducted by independent auditors retained by the company to perform an audit which meets the requirements of Government Auditing Standards or Office of Management and Budget Circular A-133 (OMB A-133).

Financial

A financial audit is performed to ascertain whether or not the financial statements are accurate and represent the activities and results undertaken by the business during the reporting period. The financial audit is conducted by a qualified, independent audit firm selected by the business.

Qualifications of an auditor include the following:

- Credentials (CPA)
- Education (Degree in Accounting and related areas)
- Training
- Industry knowledge
- Experience
- Independence

A qualified auditor must be capable of developing an audit program which encompasses the financial and managerial controls of the business and any specialized requirements associated with the structure, relationships, funding, or industry specific practices. The auditor must be able to structure and review the elements (audit program) necessary to provide reasonable assurance that the financial statements are representative of the financial position of the business.

The auditor must also be independent in perspective and interests. Independence means that the auditor, the audit firm, and related parties do not have a direct or indirect financial, personal, or other interest in the outcome of the audit – other than the audit fee. Frequently, small businesses are challenged in finding qualified audit firms which are truly independent from their operations. Many audit firms do not engage in the audit of small businesses, are not experienced in audit of firms which receive federal funding, cannot charge a fee sufficient for the firm to be retained for the audit, or have a pre-existing advisory, tax, or other relationship with the small business.

An auditor is not viewed as independent if any of the following is true:

- The auditor, his/her firm, a partner or other key member in the firm provides transactional services to the small business.
- The account manager acts as oversight on both the audit and tax or transactional activities of the small business.

- The auditor, his/her firm, a partner or other key member of the firm provides strategic or other advisory role to the business, serves as a member of the management team or board, or has an ownership stake – directly or through a related party (spouse, family member, etc.).

Audits conducted by auditors who are not independent may be viewed as defective and be rejected as fulfilling the audit requirement imposed on companies exceeding the audit threshold requirement.

A-133 (Single Audit)

The A-133 audit requires an auditor to use a risk-based approach to determine which programs are required to be reviewed. If the single audit requirement is agreed to by the small business, then the audit performed must provide assurance that the following is true:

- The financial statements are presented fairly and reflect the true financial position of operations and are presented in accordance with GAAP (generally accepted accounting principles).
- The internal controls and accounting system provide reasonable assurance that the federal awards are performed in accordance with the terms and conditions, program guidelines, and applicable laws and regulations.
- The accounting and business management systems provide reasonable control over funds and produce accurate tracking of direct costs and allocation of shared costs.
- The business is in compliance with all laws, regulations, and agreements including labor, wage, tax, and others directly included in any federal agreements or that are a part of operating a business.

Areas of review include:

- Allowable and unallowable activities
- Allocable and unallowable costs
- Cash management
- Eligibility
- Equipment
- Real property
- Matching
- Level of effort
- Period of funding
- Program income
- Procurement practices
- Reporting
- Subrecipient monitoring

Yellow Book

The Government Auditing Standards are referred to as the "Yellow Book". Government Auditing Standards contain the rules and guidance for audits of government organizations, programs, activities, and functions, and of government assistance received by contractors, nonprofit organizations, and other non-government organizations. The standards prescribe the qualifications of the auditors, the type and nature of the audit, and the content of a meaningful audit report. A "Yellow Book" audit is an audit which meets those standards.

Recordkeeping

One of the fundamental requirements for all federal fund recipients is to maintain an "adequate" system of documentation to support operational activity and financial transactions. The accounting system is the primary mechanism for identifying the types of documentation supporting each transaction. The accounting system and the accompanying paper work trail should facilitate on-going, daily activity, management and control of financial operations as well as provide sufficient records for financial and governmental audits.

Regardless of the size of the organization, for all recipients of federal funding, "adequate" recordkeeping systems have core characteristics and abilities. The selected system must be able to perform the following functions:

- record transactions in a systematic manner
- match payments to invoices and other appropriate documentation, possibly including bills of lading, purchase orders, internal authorization records, budgets, etc.
- record and identify obligation of funds – purchase orders, use of credit and debit cards, accrual of payroll and other future payments
- record receipts
- maintain cash balances on hand
- generate financial statements for each project, program, funding source, and the business
- document employee time including overtime and time-off

Time & Effort Reporting – Timekeeping

Policy, Process and Controls

Timekeeping is one of, if not the most, important transactional processes a business undertakes. The documentation of time spent and the accuracy of those records is significant in payroll, client invoicing, project charges, cost development, profitability, and compliance with numerous Federal and State regulations. Timesheets and payroll records are required as part of Department of Labor regulations, government contracting, grant programs, and as tools for understanding where your business is engaged in activities.

While expenditures on equipment can be significant, those transactions are verifiable with what is known as third-party documentation – invoices, bills of lading, and other paperwork generated outside of your business. The only source for timesheets and related documentation is your business records.

Consequently, timekeeping and time and effort reporting comes under significant, even intense scrutiny. It is imperative that an award recipient understand and meet the requirements of a "positive time and effort reporting system" – meaning a robust, comprehensive system of policy and process which properly identifies, records, reviews, monitors, tracks, controls, values, and reports actual time worked by all employees in the organization.

Timekeeping is not limited to employees involved directly with the grants or contracts. Every member of the organization – every employee, regardless of job function – must track and report actual hours worked. Time and effort reporting is the basis for the distribution of labor costs - direct and indirect – which must be accounted for in TOTAL hours. Hours worked at home, worked on the weekends, in the evenings, wherever and whenever an individual works, all must be recorded and used to determine the appropriate costs to charge to each project.

Labor costs must be tracked to the appropriate cost objective (activity, project, grant, program) whether it is internal research, government project, commercial project, or time associated with an unallowable activity. Time tracking must encompass

- Direct charges to projects
- Indirect charges to cost pools
- Unallowable costs to segregated pools

Timekeeping – time and effort reporting – emphasizes the documentation of all the activities employees are performing. Again, due to the nature of labor costs, there is no third party or external documentation which can be used as objective evidence or supporting documentation. This lack of "independent" transaction documents places additional emphasis on internal controls to ensure that individual employees recognize and fulfill their personal obligation to maintain accurate, timely, and complete records of activities. It also require that the company has an obligation to ensure those records are maintained and executed properly.

The level of effort specified in an award is documented, monitored, reported and evaluated on the basis of timesheet records. When a company cannot provide adequate documentation (properly executed timesheets) and verification of the proper use of the timesheets (tracking of time to rates, hours, and dollars charged) to a particular project and all projects and costs pools, it risks those costs being questioned and ultimately disallowed under specific awards and in total. (See section on disallowed and questioned costs.)

Timesheets

Timesheets prepared properly and in a complete and timely manner are a mandatory requirement of a robust and compliant time and effort reporting system. The actual format of the timesheet is not specified; the result and method of preparing the timesheet is, however.

Timesheets must be
- maintained consistently on a daily basis
- record time (hours or fractions of hours) on a daily basis
- record all hours worked
  - regardless of location or time of day
  - whether hours impact rate or amount paid or not
- report hours of paid time off including:
  - absence
  - holiday
  - sick leave
  - personal time
- be written in ink for manual systems
- distribute the hours worked by project
- segregate indirect activities based upon the nature of the work performed
- identify, record, and correct any errors or amendments to time in a manner that enables the original entry to be seen (for manual system no "whiteouts")
- authorize and acknowledge any amendments or corrections (for manual systems, initial any changes)
- sign all time records to certify accuracy of reporting – employee and supervisor/cognizant manager
- monitor all timekeeping records and activities
- provide corrective actions for errors, violations, and late or non-reporting of time are in place
- ensure changes or alterations of original records for number of hours recorded are controlled and reviewed
- maintain written policies and procedures
  - guidance on recording actual hours worked
  - identify minimum increment of time to be recorded (exact, tenth, quarter, half hour, etc.)
  - definition of activities and whether they are direct, indirect, unallowable…
  - list of projects to report against

- disciplinary action for careless or improper recording/reporting
- detail instructions for preparing timesheets
- specify review process by supervisor and company
- understand that the timesheet is a legal document that an employee, supervisor, management, and the company are using to track and control the activities of the business and serves to:
  - verify and certify that the time as reported by the employee reflects actual activities
  - review any alterations or amendments of time
  - ensure that only the employee records time unless the employee is absent for a significant period of time

Lea A. Strickland, MBA CMA CFM CBM

Close Out

The close out of awards varies depending upon the type of award. The objectives however are the same:

- ensure that the deliverables have been completed
- account for funds expended
- understand results achieved
- protect government interests in funded project and resulting intellectual property

Grant Closeouts

Closing a grant consists of three documents:

- final progress report
- final invention disclosure
- final financial status report

The format and content of the Final Progress Report (FPR) are specified by the agency, program, and specific award agreement. The FPR summarizes the results achieved, the progress on the scope of work, lists of publications, inventions, and other outputs from the award.

The financial status report (FSR) is the summary of all expenditures made and the financial status of the award at the end of the project. The Phase I report is due no later than 90 days after the end date of the budget/project period. The report for Phase II is due 90 days from the end of that project period end date and reports the cumulative transactions of awarded support for the entire project period.

Final invention statement (FIS) or final invention disclosure is a listing of all inventions, prototypes, first use, first concept, or reduction to practice within the scope of work of the funded project.

Failure to file any of the three documents keeps the grant "open" and the recordkeeping and audits time clock keeps ticking.

An additional item to remember is the final indirect cost filing, while not specific to the close of any single project, is required within six months of the end of each fiscal year. The final indirect cost rate applicable to your grant project is necessary to compile the true costs. Once the final rates are determined, adjustments are calculated for each grant project.

Contract Closeouts

Contract closeout is the process of completing the administrative tasks related to a project which is physically complete (services provided, products delivered, etc.). The items have been received, inspected, and accepted and all that remains is to complete the "paperwork". Typical items associated with contract closeout include:

- Verification of documentation for receipt and acceptance for the full quantity of contract items has been received.
- Verification that no claims or investigations are pending.
- Settlement of all subcontractor invoices has been made.
- Government property has been properly disposed, returned, or otherwise handled.
- Audits have been completed.
- Final invoice has been submitted for payment.

Lea A. Strickland, MBA CMA CFM CBM

Key Policies

Policies

How, who, when, why, what require consistency, control, and authority. Ensuring that transactions are properly executed and adequate oversight of activities is a critical component of doing business with government funds.

Consistency of transactions occurs when the company clearly specifies its policies and procedures, roles and responsibilities. Lines of responsibility and authority for originating transactions, making commitments (financial and other types), and executing programmatic content on time and within budget must be clear as required:

- Cost
- Audit
- Travel
- Expenses
- Procurement
- Compensation – Key Executives and Employees
- Asset management
- Intellectual property
- Subrecipient monitoring
- Timekeeping
- Recordkeeping
- Cash management
- Payments: Invoicing and draw downs
- Accounting system
- Related party transactions
- Subcontracting plan
- Contract closeout
- Grant closeout
- Ethical misconduct – research, financial, and general
- Program income

Common Mistakes, Issues, and Problems

Inadequate Accounting System

The accounting system selected will be considered inadequate when it is incapable of tracking and/or performing the following requirements:

- Track and report costs by type and by project
- Provide adequate and sufficient management controls and reviews
- Monitor to established policies, procedures, and processes
- Segregate duties
- Monitor and report adherence to plans, including budgets
- Maintain adequate cost control
- Handle costs consistently
- Generate meaningful reports
- Justify indirect cost levels
- Support direct and indirect costs with adequate documentation

Inadequate Timekeeping System

Complete, correct, and comprehensive timekeeping is a critical factor in providing required "adequate" documentation of time and effort expended. The following "mistakes" place funding in jeopardy:

- Timesheets are not maintained.
- Timesheets are not signed, dated, and/or reviewed by supervisor.
- Activities are not sufficiently identified – administrative, paid time-off, time spent on internal research projects, and other activities are not recorded.
- Actual hours worked are not recorded.
- Hours reported were not used to determine allowable charges and costs.
- Level of effort expended versus required level of effort was not monitored.
- Timekeeping used as a "minimal" verification for payroll and not for tracking and assignment of costs to projects.
- Failure to require subrecipients to keep adequate timekeeping records.

Lea A. Strickland, MBA CMA CFM CBM

Inconsistent Treatment of Costs

Regardless of the size of the company, recipients of federal money are required to treat costs consistently across the entire organization. Failure to do so may result in inappropriate shifting of costs and under review or audit lead to disallowance of costs or termination of funding.

- Costs treated as direct costs under government projects and indirect under non-government projects.
- Costs charged to government projects based upon "availability" of funds and not on the actual relationship to activities (direct) or benefits (indirect).
- All indirect costs charged to government projects because it is the "only" project the company has, instead of using the appropriate indirect cost rate.
- Costs of similar nature and purpose being treated differently period to period or project to project based upon the funding source.

Unallowable Costs

Proper accounting practices, mandatory for all federal funding, require that costs are charged correctly as under the applicable cost principles and terms of conditions of the award. These unallowable costs, both direct and indirect, must be properly excluded from charges in all cases.

- All costs associated with unallowable activities were not charged properly to the activity – including salaries, wages, benefits, and other costs.
- The share of indirect costs properly associated with direct costs were not properly charged because the underlying direct charges were not handled appropriately.
- Differences in allowability based upon special terms and conditions of specific projects or programs were not properly excluded from charges.
- Unallowable cost from specific projects, such as the loss on a project, were improperly shifted to other projects because of inadequate accounting practices.

Lea A. Strickland, MBA CMA CFM CBM

Credits

All credits, regardless of source or kind, must be accounted for against the activity which originated the cost. Applicable credits include: discounts, refunds, rebates, coupons, and other similar instruments.

▪ Due to the difference in timing between the original transactions and subsequent issuance of credits, the reduction of original cost by the credit amount is often overlooked and unreported.

Program Income

Government monies bring stipulations for the reporting of income generated by any action which is a result of the funding. Stated also is the manner in which that income must be identified and reported.

- Failure to define, identify, track, and report program income (revenues generated from the activities funded within the project) were not accounted for nor appropriately applied (additive, deductive, match, combination) to the project.
- Failure to apply program income rules to the applicable project and the business.

Indirect Cost Allocation Base

As with direct costs, indirect costs must be allocated in the manner prescribed by the funding documentation.

- Selected allocation base did not equitably distribute indirect costs to all projects.
- Indirect cost base was improperly calculated.
- Indirect cost base improperly excluded costs that should have been included resulting in a disproportionate allocation.

Expressly Unallowable Costs

Unallowable costs are just that – unallowable. They must not be charged to any part of a project.

- Costs specifically identified as unallowable or conditionally allowable where conditions were not met were charged to projects.

Lea A. Strickland, MBA CMA CFM CBM

Related Party or Inter-organizational Costs

The requirement for accurate, complete documentation and recordkeeping places an even greater responsibility on those recipients who have interests in more than one company. Whatever the interest, whatever the inclination to blur the lines of distinction between or among entities, resist it! Costs, sub-awards and/or contracts, even profits, must be kept separate, recognized, documented, and disbursed according to the terms of the award.

- Labor and other costs related to activities occurring in a related company – one that is substantially controlled, managed, or owned by the same investors, managers, etc – charged costs to projects that were not based on actual costs.
- Timekeeping records were not properly maintained.
- Sub-awards or subcontracts were made to related companies based upon relationship and not on procurement practices.
- Common or shared facilities, administrative, and other costs were apportioned based on availability of funds and not on benefits or other acceptable allocation base.
- Mark-ups and/or profits/fees were applied to supplies, materials, and other charges.

Budgets

Budgets as authorized, approved, and funded are to be followed. Any changes made in the use of funds may require prior approval of the awarding agency. Rates and fees are as awarded.

- Where required, prior approvals were not obtained to change budget amounts:
  - Increases in single line item
  - Purchase of equipment
  - Foreign subcontracts
  - Moving costs between cost categories
- Appropriate indirect rates were not used.
- Salary amounts in excess of applicable compensation ceilings were exceed.

Unsupported Costs

Recipients of government funds must maintain at all times adequate documentation as well as records of costs. Verbal authorization of changes are not considered adequate. Costs must be actual expenses incurred, obligated, and expended.

- Adequate records (receipts, timesheets, etc.) were not obtained or maintained to support expenditures made.
- Verbal approvals were relied upon for authorization from project officer.
- Modifications of award were made without authorization.
- Changes in scope, technical approach, key personnel, or other cost element without notification and/or required approvals.

Frequently Asked Questions

1. What do we do if an award does not provide any indirect costs or provides an indirect rate which is lower than those established by the provisional or final indirect rate?

    There are several governing standards regarding allocation of indirect costs:

    - Indirect costs are allocated on the basis of the approved rate and cost base.
    - Indirect costs are allocated to all projects based and any restrictions on amounts or rates, or other funding limitations are applied.
    - Indirect cost amounts in excess of the allowed amounts remain associated with the project and cannot be shifted or moved to other projects.

    Unrecovered costs must be paid for with non-federal funding sources – profits, fees, external financing, or other means.

2. When we have an approved indirect rate from one agency, will that agency help us obtain proper approval of that rate for use with other agencies?

    The business is responsible for understanding and maintaining records and methodologies in support of prior indirect rate submissions. The approving agency issuing a valid indirect cost rate agreement will generally be available to discuss their methodology and level of review of rate submissions.

3. If our final indirect rate is higher than the provisional rate, will we be able to recover the additional amount?

    This is the answer: it depends on the award, program, terms and conditions, and funding limitations. Whenever an organization receives a final rate determination which differs from the provisional rate – greater or lesser – then that adjustment should be calculated and reported to the funding agency.

4. In the event that the direct costs in an award are underspent, and the indirect cost rate exceeds the ceiling placed on indirect costs, can the direct cost be rebudgeted to recover the indirect costs?

    No. When a ceiling is placed on indirect costs rates, that ceiling is applicable regardless of any underspending on direct costs. A request for modification of the award could be made to the program office. It would, however, be subject to agency approval and any program restrictions within authorization legislation.

5. Can indirect cost proposals be calculated only on Federal projects?

   No, indirect costs rates are based on all activities of the business.

6. Are audit costs allowable?

   Yes, audit costs are allowable presuming that such costs are reasonable, necessary, etc. Audit costs may be treated as direct or indirect costs depending upon the type of audit, whether the audit is required by a specific project, etc.

7. What are the concerns of awarding agencies and the oversight or cognizant cost group about indirect cost proposal submissions?

   The primary concern of agency officials is the failure by the awardee to disclose all information or provide complete documentation in support of the proposal. These are two of the most common discrepancies:

   - Insufficient detail to explain the submission
   - Proposals are not reconcilable to project budgets and/or financial statements and contain no explanation of any differences

Lea A. Strickland, MBA CMA CFM CBM

Acronyms

A&R	Alteration and Renovation
ACH	Automated Clearinghouse
AHRQ	Agency for Healthcare Research and Quality
AoA	Administration on Aging
AOO	Authorized Organizational Official
AREA	Academic Research and Enhancement Award
CDC	Centers for Disease Control and Prevention
CFR	Code of Federal Regulations
CGMO	Chief Grants Management Officer
CMS	Centers for Medicare and Medicaid Services
CoC	Certificate of Confidentiality
COR	Contract Officer Representative
CRISP	Computer Retrieval of Information on Scientific Projects
CSR	Center for Scientific Review
DAB	Departmental Appeals Board
DCA	Division of Cost Allocation, HHS
DEA	Drug Enforcement Administration
DEOIR	Division of Extramural Outreach and Information Resources, NIH
DES	Department of Engineering Services, NIH
DFAS	Division of Financial Advisory Services, NIH
DoC	Department of Commerce
DoD	Department of Defense
DoL	Department of Labor
DPM	Division of Payment Management, HHS
DSMB	Data and Safety Monitoring Board
EA	Expanded Authorities
EO	Executive Order
eRA	Electronic Research Administration
F&A	Facilities and Administrative (costs)

FAC	Federal Audit Clearinghouse
FAR	Federal Acquisition Regulation
FCTR	Federal Cash Transactions Report (SF 272)
FDA	Food and Drug Administration
FDP	Federal Demonstration Partnership
FEMA	Federal Emergency Management Agency
FOI	Freedom of Information
FOIA	Freedom of Information Act
FSR	Financial Status Report (SF 269 or 269A)
FTR	Federal Travel Regulation
FWA	Federal-Wide Assurance
GCRC	General Clinical Research Centers
GMO	Grants Management Officer
GMS	Grants Management Specialist
GMP	Guaranteed Maximum Price
GPO	Government Printing Office
GSA	General Services Administration
HESC	Human Embryonic Stem Cells
HHS	Department of Health and Human Services
HRSA	Health Resources and Services Administration
IACUC	Institutional Animal Care and Use Committee
IBC	Institutional Biosafety Committee
IDE	Investigational Device Exception
IHS	Indian Health Service
IND	Investigational New Drug
IR&D	Independent Research and Development
IRB	Institutional Review Board
IRG	Initial Review Group
IRS	Internal Revenue Service

LWOP	Leave Without Pay
MOU	Memorandum Of Understanding
MPA	Multiple Project Assurance
NCRR	National Center for Research Resources
NEARC	National External Audit Review Center, OIG
NEI	National Eye Institute
NEPA	National Environmental Policy Act
NFI	Notice of Federal Interest
NGA	Notice of Grant Award
NICHD	National Institute for Child Health and Human Development
NIDCR	National Institute of Dental and Craniofacial Research
NIGMS	National Institute of General Medical Sciences
NIH	National Institutes of Health
NIHGPS	National Institutes of Health Grants Policy Statement
NIMH	National Institute of Mental Health
NINR	National Institute on Nursing Research
NLM	National Library of Medicine
NTIS	National Technical Information Service
OBA	Office of Biotechnology Activities, NIH
OCR	Office for Civil Rights, HHS
OER	Office of Extramural Research, NIH
OFCCP	Office of Federal Contract Compliance Programs, DoL
OFM	Office of Financial Management, NIH
OHRP	Office for Human Research Protections, HHS
OIG	Office of the Inspector General
OLAW	Office of Laboratory Animal Welfare, NIH
OMB	Office of Management and Budget
ONR	Office of Naval Research
OPERA	Office of Policy for Extramural Research Administration, NIH

OPHS	Office of Public Health and Science
ORCA	On-line Representation and Certification Application
ORI	Office of Research Integrity, HHS
PA	Program Announcement
PD	Program Director/Project Director
PHS	Public Health Service
PI	Principal Investigator
P.L.	Public Law
PMS	Payment Management System, HHS
PO	Program Official
PSC	Payback Service Center, NIH
R&D	Research and Development
RFA	Request For Applications
RFP	Request For Proposals
S&W	Salaries and Wages
SAMHSA	Substance Abuse and Mental Health Services Administration
SBA	Small Business Administration
SBC	Small Business Concern
SBIR	Small Business Innovation Research Program
SEP	Special Emphasis Panel
SF	Standard Form
SII	Successor-In-Interest
SNAP	Streamlined Non-competing Award Process
SO	Signing Official
SPOC	State Single Point of Contact
SRA	Scientific Review Administrator
SRG	Scientific Review Group
STTR	Small Business Technology Transfer Program
U.S.C.	United States Code

USDA	United States Department of Agriculture
USPS	United States Postal Service
VA	Department of Veterans Affairs
VAMC	VA Medical Center
VANPC	VA-Affiliated Non-Profit research Corporation

Glossary

Accrual-basis: recording transactions at the time of occurrence rather than at the time cash is paid out.   An example would be recording a utility bill as a liability (account payable) at the time the bill is received, or recording a sale at the time of delivery or shipment instead of when cash is received.

Accrued expenditure: charges incurred by a recipient during a given period requiring the provision of funds for any or all of the following:

- goods and other tangible property received
- services performed by employees, contractors, subrecipients, and other payees
- other amounts becoming owed under programs for which no current services or performance is required.

Accrued income:

- Sum of earnings during a given period from   services performed by the recipient and/or goods and other tangible property delivered to purchasers
- amounts becoming owed to the recipient for which no current services or performance is required by the recipient.

Additive program income: program income which must be added to funds committed to the project or program and used to further eligible project or program objectives.

Adequate evidence: information sufficient to support the reasonable belief that a particular act or omission has occurred.

Advance payment: payment made to a recipient upon its request, either before outlays are made by the recipient or through the use of predetermined payment schedules.

Affiliate: business concerns, organizations, or individuals that control each other or that are controlled by a third party.   Control may include shared management or ownership; common use of facilities, equipment, and employees; or family interest.

Allocability: A cost of an item (materials, services, etc.) is shared by a specific grant, function, department, or project (referred to as a cost objective), if the item is required by the cost objective based upon the relative benefits received or another equitable basis. A cost is allocable to a grant if it is incurred solely in order to advance work under the grant (direct cost); it benefits both the grant and other work of the institution, including other grant-supported projects (indirect cost); or it is necessary to the overall operation of the organization and is deemed to be assignable, at least in part, to the grant (indirect cost).

Alteration and renovation: work which changes the interior arrangements or other physical characteristics of an existing facility or of installed equipment so that it can be used more effectively for its currently designated purpose or adapted to an alternative use to meet a programmatic requirement. Major A&R (including modernization, remodeling, or improvement) of an existing building is permitted under an NIH grant only when the authorizing statute for the program specifically allows that activity.

Amortization: the recognition of the use of an intangible asset by the business. Amortization reduces the taxable income of a business by recognition of a non-cash expense; a means of the business recognizing the use or consumption of the value or life of the asset.

Applied research: efforts to determine and exploit the potential of science and engineering knowledge and understanding in technology such as new materials, devices, methods, and processes.

Approved budget: financial expenditure plan for the grant-supported project or activity, including revisions approved by awarding agency and permissible revisions made by the grantee. The approved budget consists of Federal (grant) funds and, if required by the terms and conditions of the award, non-Federal participation in the form of matching or cost sharing.

Asset: anything having value which can be determined by having an exchange of another asset, cash, or something of monetary value. Computers are, for example, an asset.

Assignment of claims: the transfer or making over by the contractor to a bank, trust company, or other financing institution, its right to be paid by the Government for contract performance. This is done as security for a loan to the contractor.

Award: financial assistance which provides support or stimulation to accomplish a public purpose. Awards by the Federal Government to an eligible recipient include grants and other agreements in the form of money or property in lieu of money.

Award – Active: those for which the performance period has not expired.

Award – Closed: those for which the performance period has expired; all disbursements have been made, and the final reports (financial, technical, and invention disclosures) have been submitted, accepted, and recorded by the awarding agency.

Award – Expired: those for which the performance period has expired.

Award – Open: may be either active or expired awards which have not been closed out.

Awardee: organizational entity receiving an SBIR award, either Phase I, Phase II, or Phase III.

Balance sheet: one of the three financial statements which represent the financial position of the business. Balance sheets contain the value of assets, liabilities, and equity of the business at a specified date.

Basic research: that research directed toward increasing knowledge in science. The primary aim of basic research is a fuller knowledge or understanding of the subject under study, rather than any practical application of that knowledge.

Bookkeeping: recording the transactions of the business in financial terms to reflect the activities of the business for tax, financial, and managerial reporting.

Break-even: the point where revenues/sales equal expenses. There is no profit and no loss to the business.

Budget period: intervals of time (usually 12 months each) into which a project period is divided for budgetary and funding purposes.

Budget start date: beginning date of a grant period.

Budget end date: ending date of a grant period.

Calendar Year: the actual January 1 through December 31 year.

Capacity: ability of an organization to produce a certain level of goods or services for sale.

Capital: dollars invested or available to invest in a business or other venture.

Capital equipment: equipment typically used in the production of goods or services. Capital equipment has a substantial monetary value.

Capital expenditure: amount of money spent to acquire or improve a capital asset (equipment or building).

Cash-basis: an accounting method which records transactions at the time cash is received or spent. When using a cash basis, a transaction is recorded only when a bill is paid – either a check is written or cash is exchanged, or a sale is recorded only at the time cash is received.

Cash request: Recipient act of connecting to a payment system to request funding. These funds may be requested only for immediate disbursement purposes. In general, the requested funds are delivered on a next-day basis.

Certificate of Competency: A certificate issued by the Small Business Administration (SBA) stating that the holder is "responsible" (in terms of capability, competency, capacity, credit, integrity, perseverance, and tenacity) for the purpose of receiving and performing a specific government contract.

Certified 8(a) firm: A firm owned and operated by socially and economically disadvantaged individuals and eligible to receive federal contracts under the Small Business Administration's 8(a) Business Development Program.

Change order: a written order, signed by the contracting officer, directing the contractor to amend the scope of work, specific tasks, or other aspects of the agreement.

Chart of Accounts: accounting structure of a business used to record the different types of transactions. The major categories of a chart of accounts are: assets, liabilities, equity.

Clinical research: Patient-oriented research, including epidemiologic and behavioral studies, outcomes research, and health services research.

Clinical trial: biomedical or behavioral research study of human subjects which is designed to answer specific questions about biomedical or behavioral interventions (drugs, treatments, devices, or new ways of using known drugs, treatments, or devices).

Closeout: Discontinuation of an award after services have been provided, all funds drawn from PMS, all disbursements have been made and reported on the

PSC 272, and the Final Financial Status Report (SF 269) has been submitted, accepted, recorded, and is in agreement with the advances and disbursements reflected in The Payment Management System.

Cognizant agency: the Federal agency that, on behalf of all Federal agencies, is responsible for establishing final indirect cost rates and forward pricing rates, if applicable, and administering cost accounting standards for all contracts in a business unit.

Co-investigator: an individual involved with the PI in the scientific development or execution of a project. The co-investigator (collaborator) may be employed by, or be affiliated with, the applicant/grantee organization or another organization participating in the project under a consortium agreement. A co-investigator typically devotes a specified percentage of time to the project and is considered "key personnel." The designation of a co-investigator, if applicable, does not affect the PI's roles and responsibilities.

Commercialization: phase of business where a concept, product, or service is transformed into a viable "product" for sale to consumers, businesses, institutions, or the government.

Compensation: the amount of wages, salary, benefits, and other items paid to an employee.

Contract: a legal agreement (oral or written) between two or more parties regarding the terms, conditions, actions, roles, responsibilities, deliverables, or other factors which influence or define the business relationship.

Conversion cycle: the time required for a business to convert raw materials, labor, and other inputs to a process into a different good or service available for sale.

Consent to subcontract: the contracting officer's written consent for the prime contractor to enter into a particular subcontract.

Consistency: The requirement that costs be treated the same when assigning them to cost objectives, although costs may be charged as either direct costs or F&A costs, depending on their identifiable benefit to a particular project or program. They must be treated consistently for all work of the organization under similar circumstances, regardless of the source of funding, so as to avoid duplicate charges.

Consortium: coalition of organizations, such as banks and corporations, set up to fund ventures requiring large capital resources.

Consortium agreement: formalized agreement whereby a research project is carried out by the grantee and one or more other organizations which are separate legal entities. Under the agreement, the grantee must perform a substantive role in the conduct of the planned research and not merely serve as a conduit of funds to another party or parties.

Consultant: an individual who provides professional advice or services for a fee and who is normally not an employee of the engaging party. The term "consultant" may also include firms which provide professional advice or services.

Contract: a mutually binding legal relationship obligating the seller to furnish the supplies or services (including construction) and the buyer to pay for them. It includes all types of commitments which obligate the Government to an expenditure of appropriated funds and which, except as otherwise authorized, are in writing.

Contract clause: a section of a legal agreement. A contract clause defines terms or conditions applicable to the execution and conduct of a project or relationship.

Contract modification: any written change in the terms of a contract.

Contract officer: a person with the authority to enter into, administer, and/or terminate contracts and make related determinations and findings.

Cooperative agreement: an award of financial assistance which is used to enter into the same kind of relationship as a grant; and is distinguished from a grant in that it provides for substantial involvement between the Federal agency and the recipient in carrying out the activity contemplated by the award.

Corporation: a legal and tax entity which is recognized as separate from its owners. It may enter into agreements, contracts, and other binding instruments based upon the actions of its agents, officers, employees, or directors. Corporations may be not-for-profit, for-profit, subchapter S or C.

Cost: the amount of value either exchanged for an item, calculated for an item produced, or the results of the manufacture or production process; the sum of inputs – direct and indirect, materials, labor, and overhead which a business incurs to produce a product or service.

Cost (or pricing) data: all facts which, as of the date of price agreement or, if applicable, an earlier date agreed upon between the parties which is as close as practicable to the date of agreement on price, prudent buyers and sellers would reasonably expect to affect price negotiations significantly.

Cost overrun: any amount charged in excess of the Federal share of costs for the project period (competitive segment).

Cost pool: an accounting term referring to the accumulation of common or indirect costs into a single account or group of accounts for allocation based upon an acceptable method, which may be direct costs, hours, square footage, or other basis which results in a "fair" share of costs being assigned to a particular activity, project, product, or process.

Cost principles four test: the test for allowability based upon consistency, conformance, allocability, reasonableness.

Cost share/match: an explicit arrangement under which the contractor bears some of the burden of reasonable, allocable, and allowable contract cost.

CPA (Certified Public Accountant): a person who has passed a test of a body of knowledge related to financial accounting, financial reporting, tax, and audit. This person has also (in most states) had on-the-job experience under the supervision of another CPA for a specified period of time (varies by state).

*CRADA (*Cooperative Research and Development Agreement): A Cooperative Research and Development Agreement is a legal agreement between a federal laboratory and a nonfederal party to conduct specified research or development efforts consistent with the missions of the federal laboratory. The primary purpose of a CRADA is to encourage the transfer of commercially useful technologies from federal laboratories to the private sector and to make accessible unique capabilities and facilities.

Current accounting period: a period of time chosen by the recipient for purposes of financial statements and audits.

Date of completion: date on which all work under an award is completed or the date on the award document, or any supplement or amendment thereto, on which awarding agency sponsorship ends.

Debarment: action taken by a debarring official to exclude a contractor from Government contracting and Government-approved subcontracting for a reasonable, specified period; a contractor who is excluded is "debarred."

Debt: the amount owed to another person, business, or legal entity for a good, service, or product already received or the amount due from a legally binding contract or agreement for purchase.

Deductive program income: income deducted from total allowable costs of the project or program to determine the net allowable costs on which the Federal share of costs will be based.

Defense contractor: any entity which enters into a contract with the United States for the production of material or for the performance of services for the national defense.

Delivery order: an order for supplies placed against an established contract or with Government sources.

Depreciation: the recognition of the use of an asset in the business. Depreciation reduces the taxable income of a business by recognition of a non-cash expense. It is also the means of a business recovering its investment in buildings or equipment and is intended to enable the business to "set aside" funds for replacing the equipment at a future time.

Direct cost: any cost which is identified specifically with a particular final cost objective. Direct costs are not limited to items incorporated in the end product as material or labor. Costs identified specifically with a contract are direct costs of that contract. All costs identified specifically with other final cost objectives of the contractor are direct costs of those cost objectives.

Disallowed cost: Charges to an award which the awarding agency determines to be unallowable, in accordance with the applicable Federal cost principles or other terms and conditions contained in the award.

Disbursement: Amounts paid for goods and services. Normally, federal funds are considered disbursed when checks have been released to pay for program and/or project costs.

Draw: to request grant funds for working capital, cash advance, or reimbursement on a grant, cooperative agreement, or contract.

Equipment: tangible nonexpendable personal property, including exempt property, charged directly to the award and having a useful life of more than one year and an acquisition cost of $5,000 or more per unit. Lower limits may be established, however, consistent with recipient policy.

Equity: ownership interest in the business.

Essentially equivalent work: work performed primarily under three situations:

- when substantially the same research is proposed for funding in more than one contract proposal or grant application submitted to the same Federal agency
- substantially the same research is submitted to two or more different Federal agencies for review and funding consideration
- a specific research objective and the research design for accomplishing an objective are the same or closely related in two or more proposals or awards, regardless of the funding source.

Excess cash: a Federal Cash Balance on Hand which should be returned to awarding agency.

Excess personal property: any personal property under the control of a Federal agency which the agency head determines is not required for its needs or for the discharge of its responsibilities.

Exempt property: tangible personal property acquired in whole or in part with Federal funds, where the awarding agency has statutory authority to vest title in the recipient without further obligation to the Federal government.

Expected disbursement amount: amount of disbursements the recipient expects to pay out upon the receipt of the payment.

Expendable equipment: tangible property which does not meet the $5,000 and 1 year of life requirement to be categorized as non-expendable equipment.

Facilities: the buildings, offices, and equipment of the businesses operations.

Facilities and administrative costs (F&A): costs which are incurred by a grantee for common or joint objectives and cannot be identified specifically with a particular project or program. These costs also are known as "indirect costs".

Fast track: a process designed to facilitate the transition from Phase I to Phase II and address "funding gaps" which frequently occur under "normal" SBIR processes. Not all agencies have Fast Track programs.

Feasibility: the practical extent to which a project can be performed successfully.

Federal acquisition regulations (FAR): established to codify uniform policies for acquisition of supplies and services by executive agencies.

Federal awarding agency: Federal agency which provides an award to the recipient.

Federal cash on hand: the amount of federal cash the recipient has on hand at the time of the request. Essentially, this is the difference between what they have drawn and what they have spent.

Federal cash transactions report (PSC 272 Report): grantees are required to file this report within 45 days after the end of each quarter. Because it is a cumulative report, the only available report will always be for the period through the last quarter.

Federal funds authorized: the total amount of Federal funds obligated by the Federal Government for use by the recipient. This amount may include any authorized carryover of unobligated funds from prior funding periods when permitted by agency regulations or agency implementing instructions

Federal share of real property, equipment or supplies: the percentage of acquisition costs for properties or supplies and any improvement expenditures paid with Federal funds.

Final indirect cost rate: the indirect cost rate established and agreed upon by the Government and the contractor as not subject to change – usually established after the close of the contractor's fiscal year (unless the parties decide upon a different period) to which it applies.

Financial assistance: transfer of a thing of value from a Federal agency to a recipient to carry out a public purpose of support or stimulation authorized by a law of the United States: grants, cooperative agreements, loans, loan guarantees, interest subsidies, insurance, food commodities, direct appropriations, and transfers of property in place of money.

First article: a preproduction model, initial production sample, test sample, first lot, pilot lot, or pilot models.

Fiscal Year: the period of operation that a business designates for its financial year which results from a business reason.

Fixture: a piece of equipment or other asset attached to a building or other capital asset.

Forecast: the forward projection of financial or operational activity based upon historical information, assumptions of future activity, economic indicators, and other factors.

Funding: how a business obtains its initial capital and subsequent investment from debt and equity holders, as well as the cash inflow from operations (sales).

Funding agreement: Any contract, grant, or cooperative agreement entered into between any Federal agency and any SBC for the performance of experimental, developmental, or research work, including products or services, funded in whole or in part by the Federal Government

Funding period: period of time when Federal funding is available for obligation by the recipient.

GAAP (Generally Accepted Accounting Principles): the "standard" way of recording business transactions in the United States.

General ledger: the summary of all transactions that occur in a company.

General ledger account: an account which contains, in summary and detail, the financial results of similar transactions.

Government cash-on-hand: amount of Federal cash actually received by the grant recipient less the Federal share of disbursements as reported.

Grant: a legal instrument used to enter into a relationship, the principal purpose of which is to transfer a thing of value to the recipient to carry out a public purpose of support or stimulation authorized by a law of the United States, rather than to acquire property or services for the government's direct benefit or use. Further, it is a relationship in which substantial involvement is not expected between the awarding agency and the recipient when carrying out the activity contemplated by the grant.

Grants officer: an official with the authority to enter into, administer, and/or terminate grants or cooperative agreements.

Income statement: the basic financial statement which reflects the results of operations over a specified period, usually one year; and reports the bottom-line profit or loss for the business during the period reported. Also called a profit and loss statement or P&L statement.

Incurred cost proposal: annual submission required by some agencies on the actual indirect costs incurred and calculation of the indirect rate(s) for the period fiscal period in which federally funded (grant, co-operative agreements, contracts) work was performed.

Indirect cost: any cost not directly identified with a single final cost objective, but identified with two or more final cost objectives or with at least one intermediate cost objective.

Indirect cost rate: the percentage or dollar factor which expresses the ratio of indirect expense incurred in a given period to direct labor cost, manufacturing cost, or another appropriate base for the same period (see also "final indirect cost rate").

Infrastructure: the operational "bones" of the business. It includes people, equipment, and facilities, as well as the "how" of operations – policies, procedures, etc.

Innovative agreement: broad authority granted DARPA to channel its support through a variety of legal instruments and flexible arrangements to support research and development activities.

Interest earned on federal funds advances: Interest earned on advances of Federal funds held by recipient.

Journal entry: a transaction in the accounting system to move, adjust, or otherwise modify the existing account balances or transactions, or to correct or properly record an activity in the financial records of the business.

Key personnel: The principal investigator (PI) and other individuals who contribute to the scientific development or execution of a project in a substantive, measurable way, whether or not they receive salaries or compensation under the grant. Consultants also may be considered key personnel if they meet this definition.

Ledger: a group of accounts recording financial transactions of a governmental unit or other organization. A ledger is a summary of transactions reflecting the accounts affected.

Liability: claims on assets which represent a remaining ownership interest by another party; the amount of money owed in exchange for a good or a service, i.e., salaries or wages owed or an invoice for merchandise purchased.

Loan: an agreement in which a lender provides funds to an individual or business. The agreement requires the borrower to make periodic payments comprised of interest (charge for the use of the funds) and principal (recovery of the loaned amount).

Matching program income: monies used to satisfy all or part of the non-Federal share of a project or program

Milestones: indicators – financial, dates, or other measurable units – which provide point-in-time references as to where a business (or individual) is in relation to a selected plan.

Monitoring: A process whereby the programmatic and business management performance aspects of a grant are assessed by reviewing information gathered from various required reports, audits, site visits, and other sources.

Notice of grant award: a legally binding document which notifies the grantee and others that an award has been made. A notice of grant award contains or references all terms and conditions of the award, and documents the obligation of Federal funds. The award notice may be in letter format and may be issued electronically.

Novation agreement: a legal instrument by which, among other things, the transferor guarantees performance of the contract, the transferee assumes all obligations under the contract, and the Government recognizes the transfer of the contract and related assets.

Obligations: the amounts of orders placed, contracts and grants awarded, services received and similar transactions during a given period which require payment by the recipient during the same or a future period.

Officer: a legal representative of a business who may act as an agent and has legal responsibility for the conduct and activities of the business.

Opportunity Cost: the "cost" of the next best option a business could undertake to generate a return on investment; the highest price or rate of return that could be generated from an alternative course of action.

Organizational conflict of interest: a situation in which a person is unable or potentially unable to perform specific work or provide assistance because of other activities or relationships with other persons. In addition, an organizational conflict of interest may occur because a person's objectivity may be impaired or an unfair competitive advantage may exist.

Other support: financial resources, whether Federal or non-Federal, commercial or organizational, available in direct support of an individual's research endeavors, including, but not limited to, research grants, cooperative agreements, contracts, or organizational awards. Other support does not include training awards, prizes, or gifts.

Outlays: Charges made to the project or program which may be reported on a cash or accrual basis.

Overtime: time worked by a contractor's employee in excess of the employee's normal workweek or workday (depends upon state regulations).

Overtime premium: the difference between the contractor's regular rate of pay to an employee for the shift involved and the higher rate paid for overtime. It does not include shift premium, i.e., the difference between the contractor's regular rate of pay to an employee and the higher rate paid for extra-pay shift work.

Partial termination: termination of a part, but not all, of the work which has not been completed and accepted under a contract.

Personal Liability: the financial and other obligations which may arise from activity, decisions, or actions of an individual in his/her role as an employee, officer, or agent of a business or as an individual. There are some activities which cannot be shielded through the creation of a corporation or other separate legal entity under which business is conducted.

Phase I: the startup phase. Typically awards of up to $100,000 for approximately 6 months support exploration of the technical merit or feasibility of an idea or technology

Phase II: the feasibility, product development, prototyping, and evaluation of commercial potential phase. Typically awards range up to $750,000 and for a period up to 2 years. Phase II expands Phase I results. Only Phase I award winners are considered for Phase II.

Phase II continuation: the availability of additional funds from a set-aside which an agency may provide to a Phase II recipient based upon the submission of a brief proposal related to the next stage of R&D work (usually commercialization).

Phase III: the commercial sale of government funded technology or its outcomes to non-SBIR government programs or commercial entities.

Physical Assets: equipment, furniture, or fixtures which can be seen, touched, acquired, destroyed, etc.

Policy: a written guideline of a business which establishes the proper conduct or activity for individuals within the organization.

Policy Manual: a comprehensive document which encompasses the policies of an organization across functional areas.

Pre-award survey: an evaluation of a prospective contractor's capability to perform a proposed contract.

Predetermined rate: ate is a permanent rate established for a specified period (current or future) and cannot be changed or adjusted after the fact. The rate is typically used on awards where costs to be incurred are reasonably assured and not likely to exceed the organization's actual costs.

Prime contract: a contract awarded directly by the Federal government.

Principal investigator: an individual designated by the grantee to direct the project or activity being supported by the grant. S/he is responsible and accountable to the grantee and the awarding agency for the proper conduct of the project or activity.

Prior approval: written approval from the designated GMO required for specified post-award changes in the approved project or budget. Such approval must be obtained before undertaking the proposed activity or spending.

Procurement contract: legal agreement where the principal purpose of the instrument is to acquire (purchase, lease or barter) property or services for the direct benefit or use

Pro Forma Financial Statements: forecasted financial statements.

Procedure: the "how-to" steps of an activity or task.

Profit: the difference between the total revenues and the total expenses of a business. Profit is determined by subtracting the cost of goods/services sold, operating expense, interest, depreciation and amortization, and taxes from revenues.

Program: coherent assembly of plans, project activities, and supporting resources contained within an administrative framework. The purpose of a program is to implement an organization's mission or some specific program-related aspect of that mission. For the NIHGPS, "program" refers to those NIH programs which carry out its missions through the award of grants or cooperative agreements to other organizations.

Program income: gross income earned by a grantee which is generated directly by the grant-supported project or activity or earned as a result of the award. It includes but is not limited to income from fees for services performed, the use or rental of real or personal property acquired under federally-funded projects, the sale of commodities or items fabricated under an award, license fees and royalties on patents and copyrights, and interest on loans made with award funds. Interest earned on advances of Federal funds is NOT program income. Except as otherwise provided in Federal awarding agency regulations or the terms and conditions of the award, program income does not include the receipt of principal on loans, rebates, credits, discounts, etc. or interest earned on any of these items.

Program solicitation: a formal solicitation for proposals whereby a Federal agency notifies the small business community of its R/R&D needs and interests in broad and selected areas, as appropriate to the agency, and requests proposals from SBC's in response to these needs and interests.

Progress report: periodic, usually annual, report submitted by the grantee and used by agency to assess progress and, except for the final progress report of a project period, to determine whether to provide funding for the budget period subsequent to that covered by the report.

Project period: total time for which the support of a project has been programmatically approved. The total project period comprises the initial competitive segment, any subsequent competitive segments resulting from a competing continuation award, and non-competing extensions.

Procurement records: receipts, requirements documents, technical specifications, purchase orders, and invoices.

Reasonableness: determination that the costs or actions in a particular situation are those which a prudent person would have spent or taken. A cost may be considered reasonable if the nature of the goods or services acquired or applied and the associated dollar amount reflects the actions of a prudent person under similar circumstances prevailing when the decision was made. The cost principles elaborate on this concept and address considerations such as whether the cost is of a type generally necessary for the organization's operations or the grant's performance, whether the recipient complied with its established organizational policies in incurring the cost or charge, and whether the individuals responsible for the expenditure acted with due prudence in carrying out their responsibilities to the Federal government and the public at large as well as to the organization.

Recipient: an organization receiving financial assistance directly from an awarding agency to carry out a project or program.

Request for proposal (RFP): used in negotiated procurements to communicate requirements to prospective contractors and to solicit proposals for the products and services. The requested proposals are evaluated according to various selection criteria, which may include many other factors in addition to price.

Request for quote (RFQ): a solicitation document used to obtain price, delivery, and other information from prospective contractors.

Responsible audit agency: the agency which is responsible for performing all required contract audit services at a business unit.

Revenue: the sales dollars generated by a business.

SBIR data rights: a royalty-free license for the Government, including its support service contractors, to use, modify, reproduce, release, perform, display, or disclose technical data or computer software generated and delivered under this contract for any United States government purpose.

SBIR technical data rights: rights a small business concern obtains in data generated during the performance of any SBIR Phase I, Phase II, or Phase III award which an awardee delivers to the Government during or upon completion of a Federally-funded project. The Government receives a license for this data.

Small business concern: a business that, on the date of award for of a grant, contract, or other funding activity, meets all legislative requirements to qualify as a small business. The primary requirements are:

- organized for profit
- with a place of business located in the United States
- operating primarily within the United States or making a significant contribution to the United States economy through payment of taxes or use of American products, materials or labor
- structured in the legal form of a sole proprietorship, partnership, limited liability company, corporation, joint venture, association, trust or cooperative,
- is at least 51 percent owned and controlled by one or more individuals who are citizens of, or permanent resident aliens in, the United States
- has, including its affiliates, not more than 500 employees.

Solicitation: any request to submit offers or quotations to the government for the purpose of acquiring products and services.

Statement of cash flows: a basic financial statement which reflects the changes in cash (funds) by identifying the sources and uses of the funds during the reporting period. Also called a statement of changes in financial position.

Statement of work: description of the tasks to be performed.

Sub-award: award of financial assistance in the form of money, or property in lieu of money, made under an award by a recipient to an eligible subrecipient or by a subrecipient to a lower tier subrecipient.

Subcontract: any agreement, other than one involving an employer-employee relationship, entered into by an awardee of a funding agreement calling for supplies or services for the performance of the original funding agreement.

Subrecipient: The legal entity to which a sub-award is made and which is accountable to the recipient for the use of the funds provided.

Supplies: all personal property excluding equipment, intangible property, debt instruments, and inventions of a contractor conceived or first actually reduced to practice in the performance of work under a funding agreement.

Suspension: a post-award action by the awarding agency which temporarily withdraws the agency's financial assistance sponsorship under an award, pending corrective action by the recipient or a decision to terminate the award.

Termination: cancellation of awarding agency sponsorship, in whole or in part, under an agreement at any time prior to the date of completion.

Termination for convenience: exercise of the Government's right to terminate performance of work under a contract, either completely or partially, when it is in the Government's interest.

Termination for default: the exercise of the Government's right to completely or partially terminate a contract because of the contractor's actual or anticipated failure to perform its contractual obligations.

Termination inventory: any property purchased, supplied, manufactured, furnished, or otherwise acquired for the performance of a contract subsequently terminated and properly allocable to the terminated portion of the contract. It includes Government-furnished property. It does not include any facilities, material, special test equipment, or special tooling which are subject to a separate contract or to a special contract requirement governing their use or disposition.

Terms and conditions: all legal requirements imposed on a grant by the awarding agency, whether based on statute, regulation, policy, or other document referenced in the grant award, or specified by the grant award document itself.

Third-party in-kind contributions: the value of non-cash contributions provided by non-Federal third parties.

Total project costs: total allowable costs (both direct costs and F&A costs) incurred by the grantee to carry out a grant-supported project or activity.

Transactions: the exchange of money for goods or services; the exchange of one good or service for other goods or services.

Unallowable costs: any cost which, under the provisions of any pertinent law, regulation, or contract, cannot be included in prices, cost-reimbursements, or settlements under a Government contract to which it is allocable.

Unliquidated obligation: For financial reports prepared on a cash basis, the amount of obligations incurred by the recipient which have not been paid. For reports prepared on an accrual basis, the amount of obligations incurred by the recipient for which an outlay has not been recorded.

Unobligated balance: the portion of funds authorized by an awarding agency that have not obligated by the recipient. The unobligated balance is determined by deducting the cumulative obligations from the cumulative funds authorized.

Unrecovered indirect cost: the difference between the amount awarded and the amount which could have been awarded under the recipient's approved negotiated indirect cost rate.

Unsolicited proposal: a written proposal submitted to an agency on the initiative of the offeror for a new or innovative idea that is for the purpose of obtaining a contract with the Government. An unsolicited proposal is not in response to a request for proposals, Broad Agency Announcement, Small Business Innovation Research topic, Small Business Technology Transfer Research topic, Program Research and Development Announcement, or any other Government-initiated solicitation or program.

Vendor: a seller of a good or service.

Working capital advance: a procedure which advances funds to the recipient to cover estimated disbursement needs for a specified initial period.

Yellow book: name used for Government Auditing Standards. The Yellow Book contains standards for audits of government organizations, programs, activities, and functions, and of government assistance received by contractors, nonprofit organizations, and other non-government organizations.

About the Author

 Lea A. Strickland, MBA CMA CFM CBM is President/CEO and founder of F.O.C.U.S.™ Resource, Inc., a strategic business consulting firm headquartered in the Research Triangle Park region of North Carolina. She is a nationally recognized expert on entrepreneurship and business growth issue. Lea's clients include for-profit (service and manufacturing) in traditional and emerging/growth industries (technology, life science, bio-tech, info-tech, medical device, energy, electronics, psychology, training and incentives, pharmaceutical); not-for-profit (research, business incubators, membership, trade); and institutional/government organizations. Lea is a consultant, keynote speaker, columnist (over 400 published articles), and author (Out of the Cubicle and Into Business (2005) and co-author of One Great Idea (2007) and Marketing Strategies (2007)). Lea's practical approach and advice garnered appearances in four issues of *Entrepreneur*™ *Magazine* addressing start-up, growth, and management topics. She currently publishes three newsletters: F.O.C.U.S.™ on Business, F.O.C.U.S.™ on Commercialization, and F.O.C.U.S.™ on SBIR Recipients. She can be reached at

Lea@FOCUSResourcesInc.com

919.234.3960

Printed in the United States
74753LV00002B/541-591